GREAT GAMES for GREAT PARTIES

GREAT GAMES for GREAT PARTIES

How to Throw a Perfect Party

Andrea Campbell

Illustrated by Sanford Hoffman

 Sterling Publishing Co., Inc.   New York

Library of Congress Cataloging-in-Publication Data

Campbell, Andrea.
    Great games for great parties : how to throw a perfect party /
Andrea Campbell.
        p.   cm.
    Includes index.
    ISBN 0-8069-8318-3
    1. Entertaining. 2. Games. 3. Indoor games.   I. Title.
GV1471.C16   1991
793.2—dc20   91-22983
                                                                    CIP

10 9 8 7 6 5 4 3 2 1

Published in 1991 by Sterling Publishing Company, Inc.
387 Park Avenue South, New York, N.Y. 10016
©1991 by Andrea Campbell
Distributed in Canada by Sterling Publishing
c/o Canadian Manda Group, P.O. Box 920, Station U
Toronto, Ontario, Canada M8Z 5P9
Distributed in Great Britain and Europe by Cassell PLC
Villiers House, 41/47 Strand, London WC2N 5JE, England
Distributed in Australia by Capricorn Link Ltd.
P.O. Box 665, Lane Cove, NSW 2066

Sterling ISBN 0-8069-8318-3

This book is dedicated to my husband, Michael, and to my children, Courtney and Jordan, all of whom have taught me to be an enthusiastic game player.

ACKNOWLEDGMENTS

This book would still be just an outline had it not been for the loving support of my mother and mentor, Anna Potantus.

I also want to acknowledge the support of my exchange-student daughter, Ana Perez Rivero, whose help freed me up to work on this book.

A special acknowledgment goes to my friend Alice English, a patient reader who helped me to see details in the manuscript from a new perspective. And a tip of the hat to Keith Noble, my computer tutor.

I must also mention all the people and clubs who not only provided input but who let me use them as "subjects" for trying out games: Wilma Flud and Village Writers, Xi Beta Kappa and Sigma chapters of Beta Sigma Phi, the Mis Amigas of the Extension Homemaker's Club, the Couples Club at Prince of Peace Church, and the Dobschas and their friends.

In addition, I want to thank Helen Ball for her help with the Bunko rules, Peggy Scott for the samples for the Shogum game, and Ms. Long and her class at Fountain Lake School for their ingenious work.

At Sterling, I'd like to recognize Sheila Anne Barry for having faith in my project, Sanford Hoffman for his wonderful drawings, and my editor Laurel Ornitz for her advice and kind support.

CONTENTS

	Introduction	11
1	Party Planning	13
2	Creating the Atmosphere	25
3	Leadership Qualities & Techniques	35
4	Motivating Your Guests	45
5	Pre-Party Games, Contests & Icebreakers	55
6	Quiet Games & Table Games	79
7	Relays, Musical Activities & Stunts	95
8	Shower & Pairing Games, Hunts & Events	109
9	Party Supplies & Sample Plan	123
10	Party Themes	129
11	Prizes & Gifts	143
	Games by Category	153
	Index	157

INTRODUCTION

The aim of this book is to help you develop a better understanding of what makes a good games party. It's a challenge to put on a good party, where people interact, play games, and compete with each other for fun. A certain amount of skill is required to be the kind of games leader who can present ideas and motivate people to join in. This book will help you develop these skills, and will give you over a hundred games to choose from.

When I set out on my research for this book, I discovered that most available books on game playing either were written for children, were incomplete, or were simply outdated. That firmed up my resolution to write a comprehensive, up-to-date party-games book specifically for adults that could be used for or adapted to any social function.

Parties are for people. Certainly for people to feel that they belong, you must be aware of all the nuances that go into making a party a true "people" event.

I have been fortunate in having been able to develop my own party-making skills over the last decade, planning and hosting parties for a variety of people. For instance, as an area representative for a worldwide student-exchange program, it has been my happy responsibility to host parties for the students and their American "families" in my area as part of their learning experience together. I have also had the pleasure of being a member of, and at one time the social chairperson for, a sorority. Ten years' involvement with this highly social group of women has enabled me to garner many fabulous ideas for meetings and parties. But if there's one thing I can say I've learned from my experience of planning and hosting parties, it's that nothing can bring people together faster than game playing.

Spending time enjoying ourselves with friends is one of the nicest things we can do for our own mental health and for the happiness of others. I hope this book will enhance that enjoyment.

1
PARTY PLANNING

Good parties are not automatic. It is not enough to get a room filled with people, feed them, and then expect them to have fun. Generally, when people are invited into strange territory (meaning, not their own home environment), they have a tendency to be self-conscious and inhibited. The guests do not mean to be unresponsive; they just do not know what is expected of them. But if you provide the correct conditions, the right set of circumstances, your guests will interact spontaneously. Your goal then, for a memorable gathering, is to get them to respond and interact with each other for good fun. There are no magic formulas to bring this about, however; it just takes creative step-by-step planning.

I'm not suggesting that the ideas presented in this book are the only ways to get people to interact with each other and achieve success. The book is meant to be a guide—feel free to adapt these suggestions according to your own common sense and the special needs and interests of your guests. Delight in the creativity and in the social creature within yourself.

THE SETTING AND MOOD

Atmosphere has a lot to do with the way we react to the people around us. This response to our surroundings is inherent in our personality whether we are conscious of it or not. An atmosphere that is conducive to people being engaged in friendship can be easily created—this is a fact that will be illustrated many times over in this book.

Think about one of your favorite restaurants. Perhaps it is an elegant place where you go to celebrate special occasions such as a birthday or anniversary. Now think about what makes this restaurant so special for you. Is the lighting subdued and romantic? Are there fresh flowers or towering shiny trees and plants? Do

13

you feel at home in the period decor, or do you like the cushiony feeling of the thick Persian rugs under your feet? Does the music create the right backdrop for dining or conversation? Are the waiters and hosts attentive to your needs?

You know that whether your favorite haunt is an expensive French restaurant or a quiet rustic inn, it's the ambiance that calls to you. The carefully planned atmosphere of the establishment is the all-deciding element that attracts you and makes you want to return.

Since you probably do not have the resources of your favorite restaurant to convey a mood, you will be happy to learn that a successful atmosphere for a party is not determined by the size of your bank account. For a game players' party, it is the camaraderie generated, along with some special or unusual touches, that will create an atmosphere where there's interest and excitement.

The atmosphere of a party is established before the first guests arrive. The invitations will be the first step towards achieving a mood and the mood will continue until you close the door after the last guest has left.

The atmosphere of your party will largely depend on you. It's a big job but not too big with some planning beforehand and some answers to the key questions that follow.

QUESTIONS TO ASK YOURSELF
. . . .

GUESTS
- Who are the people whom you will invite? Is this a neighborhood group, a sorority, a church or temple membership gathering, the PTA organizing committee, coworkers?
- How many will be coming?
- Will there be the same amount of women as men?
- Do you have special connections with them?
- Are there any restrictions or preconditions to consider?
- Do these people know each other?
- Why are you getting together? Is this a celebration for your spouse's promotion, a surprise birthday party, or perhaps a bon voyage for an old friend?

TIME
- When will you have it?
- Will it be near or on a holiday?
- What will the season be and how will people be dressed?

- Have you thought about the time of day? Would a Sunday afternoon be better than a Friday night for this group?

THEME
- Were you thinking of having a picnic or perhaps a party at a lake?
- Maybe this is a gathering to play cards or Bunko? With dancing?
- Do you want to create an Olympics of your own design for a hot summer day?
- Is there some kind of theme you can incorporate into the planning for a special or surprise element?
- Exactly what type of party did you have in mind?

LOCATION
- Do you have a place in mind?
- Will your patio garden be the perfect spot?
- What about the church fellowship hall or maybe the school auditorium?
- Is there a community room or pool available in your apartment complex?

FACILITIES
- Think about space. The facilities must be sufficient for parking and the lavatory.
- What about other needs, such as:
  - hanging coats?
  - controlling electricity and heat?
  - ample tables and chairs?
  - a public address system for announcements?
  - waste cans and receptacles?
  - a dance floor?
  - a fireplace or grills for cooking?
  - a piano?
- Will you have access to the building early?
- Are there any regulations?
- Do you need a reservation for the room, and is a deposit required?
- Will you need to draw up maps?

COST
- Will you need to budget for decorations, refreshments, and/or prizes?
- Or, can you make the decorations with a committee?

- Can you make your own invitations?
- Would it be a good idea to have guests bring dishes for a potluck or their own picnic basket?
- Can the gifts be donated? Or how about a white-elephant exchange or even gag gifts?
- Can you ask people to bring things, such as drinks?
- Will you charge a few dollars per couple to make it extra nice or to be able to provide special entertainment?

Once you have answered these questions, you will be able to visualize your needs and expectations better.

If you are to be the host and it is your party alone, you can now better delegate duties to other family members or close friends who will act as assistants, because now you have a plan.

If this event is planned as a group, office, or organization function, you can also use the answers to these questions to help divide up the responsibilities among various committees. There will be something for everyone to do, not just the "creative" types. So if someone says "But I can't make invitations and my cakes are flops," he or she can be a greeter or answer the door, help to clean up, or be the person to lock up.

Your consideration of the group's interests is also very important. For instance, if the gathering is to take place at the beginning of a convention and you want the participants to get off on a lively and anticipatory footing, "get-acquainted" and "icebreaker" games would probably be in order. I sometimes think that if our politicians took part in gaming sessions before convening, they wouldn't be so defensive and consequently would get more work and legislation done.

INVITATIONS

With so much of today's mail addressed to "Occupant," how nice it is to find a handmade greeting card with a simply written note or to discover a party invitation that was created just for you. Not to steal any thunder from the professional greeting card companies, but I believe that handmade invitations are the best way to show someone that you really care. There are literally hundreds of ways to announce a party or event. An invitation made with a touch of ingenuity or perhaps cleverly picking up on the party's theme will not be thrown away with all the anonymous mail!

Over the years I have made a habit of collecting cards and invitations. Now I have started to save unusual clippings from magazines and newspapers that pass before my eyes. I squirrel away these snippets in a file folder in my art-supply cupboard, and then when I need to design an invitation of my own, I pull them out for ideas and inspiration. It's fun to sort through an idea folder and it also makes thinking up a theme for a party a lot easier. Use construction paper—it's cheap and it can be cut into various shapes to resemble a theme article, and then the details can be drawn in with soft-tipped pens. Here are some examples of theme articles for invitations:

- ice cream cone or sundae shapes for an Ice Cream Social
- brown-paper-bag baked potatos for a Potato Topping Fest
- teacup silhouettes for an old-fashioned Victorian Tea
- football cutouts (with team logo) for a Superbowl or Tailgate party
- popcorn boxes for a Film Review gathering
- harlequin masks covered with glitter for your own Mardi Gras
- large tickets that have "Admit" stamped on them (see the pattern on page 19)
- cowboy boots or Stetson hats for a gambling or Poker party, or for drinks at the local "saloon"

Invitations that reflect your theme are great fun to make as well as to receive. I was once invited to a Pirate's Dig party and the invitation was written on rolled-up parchment paper and hand-delivered in a cork-sealed brown bottle. Some additional ideas are:

- an invitation to a garden party with a seed packet on the cover—with the planting instructions really directions on how to get to the event, the time, and other details
- a scroll invitation penned in elaborate calligraphy for a Medieval Dinner
- an invitation to a Skate and Pizza Party that is made to look like pizza—and delivered in a real pizza box!

For those of you who are computer enthusiasts, many different types of software are available that you can use for designing invitations. The programs usually have a variety of fonts and a good selection of graphics.

In addition, many books of public-domain art are on the market that can be photocopied or scanned. These books include designs and motifs in lots of different styles, such as Art Deco and Victorian, and cover a large variety of topics. For instance, there are pictures of food and drink, holiday designs, and all kinds of silhouettes and borders.

You can also purchase stamp sets with different colored ink pads. Some include a complete set of the alphabet, in a couple of different styles, and a broad range of subject matter is available. I use rubber stamps with cats, leaves, a shamrock, clouds, celes-

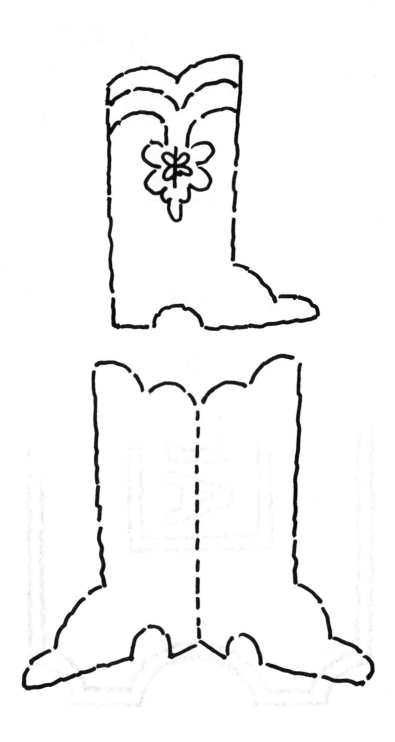

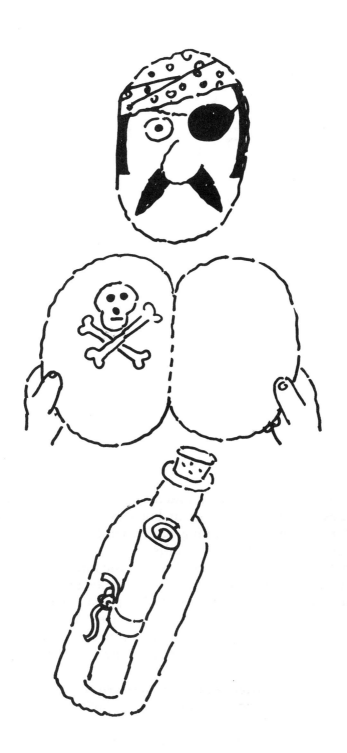

tial stars, a dog's paw print, and an Easter egg, as well as many other designs. They make great borders on cards and are also good for decorating wrapping paper. Give them a try—I think you'll be pleased with your results.

Your invitation should include this basic information: the date, time, place, dress, and R.S.V.P. You may also need to state whether the guest should bring another guest or a particular item and if a contribution of some sort is required. The R.S.V.P. on the bottom of invitations stands for the French phrase "*Respondez-vous S'il Vous Plait.*" In English, this simply translates to "Respond Please."

As a rule, invitations should be *received* at least one week in advance of the function. However, for today's busy families, two or three weeks' advance notice of a party is actually better.

As a surprise touch for a special event, you might consider

having the invitations hand-delivered. For a neighborhood party, hand delivery is especially convenient, besides being a treat for the recipient. I have heard of someone dressed as a "Care Bear" delivering an invitation promising an evening of heart-felt fun. A balloon delivered by a clown would be cute, and now there are flower shops and concessions in malls that can seal your invitations *inside* the balloons.

If you are planning a major event that calls for publicity, such as a charity ball, you might think about making posters in addition to the invitations. Posting announcements or using a newspaper article advertisement or a spot on the radio can also serve to build up excitement and lend impact to your party. However, make sure that these announcements, in whatever form they take, restate the time, place, and other particulars.

One last thought on invitations: If you happen to be inviting new people to a party or event, remember to provide a map or at least written instructions on how to reach the premises. People who have been driving around lost for hours will not be in much of a mood for a party.

2
CREATING THE ATMOSPHERE

As already mentioned, the atmosphere or the mood of a place is extremely important.

Right now as I flash back to places in my past, I can vividly remember the scene of my first brush with the social graces—a sixth-grade dance class. One reason that this memory stands out to this day is because the experience was so uncomfortable. Although I was wearing my first pair of nylon stockings, shoes with small heels, and gloves, the primary discomfort that I felt was not due to the dress code but rather to the setup of the room. The environment was all wrong. We dance-ignorant subjects stood blinking at each other in the glare of extremely bright and revealing gym lights. Lines of chairs, in straight rows like sentinels of soldiers, hugged the walls on opposite sides of the room. Of course, all the girls congregated on one side of the room and the boys (dressed in their first suits and ties) were huddled on the other. The object of this encounter was for the boys to somehow navigate the tremendous chasm created by the setting and ask a girl to be their partner for a dance. Needless to say, nearly everybody felt intimidated.

Now that we are all removed from the painful incidents of adolescence, we can breathe a sigh of relief and create our own environment for social events. This chapter is designed to give you some tips and insights into just what constitutes an enjoyable atmosphere for entertaining.

THE LOCATION

• •

Exactly where your party is going to be held is your first major concern in creating atmosphere, and your options are as varied as the resources in your community. For instance, I hosted an exchange-student family Christmas party in a bank community room in my town. I made arrangements with the bank's public relations office to reserve (no pun intended) the room for us. Although it was bank policy to loan the room out to private groups only during the week, I asked the bank, in writing, if it was possible to amend that rule so that we could have our function there on a Saturday night. In my letter I also assured them that we would leave the facilities spotless, and pick up and return the keys during bank business hours. A follow-up phone call found them more than happy to accommodate our group.

Another time I arranged permission to use my church's fellowship room, a wonderfully large space with tables and chairs and a well-equipped kitchen. Both of these places, the church and the bank rooms, were completely free of charge. I just made sure that we followed the rules set by the administrators and left the area swept and clean.

I live in a planned community in the Ouachita Mountains in Arkansas. One of the nicest parties I have every year is at the community's lake-pavilion area. Picnic tables and benches are set up under a protective canopy, and about fifty feet of grassy shore lies between the lake and the picnic tables, so I don't have to worry about little tots wandering off and playing too close to the water. There are also a rustic, smoky brick grill and fireplace along the entrance wall, with lavatory facilities at the other end. The community association has even provided a net and ball for volleyball, which is played on a grassy area across a small bridge. The pavilion has electrical outlets and lights, and large waste receptacles and dumpsters are nearby.

Planned communities are not the only living situations with a community room or recreational area available for private use. Many large apartment and condominium complexes have them.

You also might think about reserving a skating rink or a swimming pool. We have a roller rink in our downtown area and I have used it for a Skate and Pizza Party. The manager welcomes group business and he gives reduced rates on the skates and fees for parties.

You may have friends who have the perfect setting for your next get-together. Friends of ours have a ranch, where one year we had a smashing Halloween party. We decorated the porch with black and orange crepe-paper streamers and hung candy-filled "ghosts" on the clothesline for the children. Our friends provided a horse-riding exhibition and we watched a barrel race and had a pumpkin-decorating contest in which we used black soft-tipped pens instead of knives. We cooked our hot dog and chili supper over a bonfire and then we went on a hayride, complete with spooks and ghosts. The hay wagon was actually a jeep, pulling a long-bed trailer filled with hay, and the route was well plotted out. Our friends' teenaged son and his friends were hiding behind a tombstone in a nearby cemetery, and when our hay wagon pulled up, the boys jumped out and surprised all the riders in the dark. When we came back to the ranch, we toasted marshmallows on the end of sticks over the fire and had hot chocolate while sitting around the glowing embers.

IMPORTANT DETAILS
• •

Whether you are having a banquet, a picnic, or a ball, after you choose the location, there are some details to consider.

Genie Laborde is a communications consultant for a major corporation and in her book, *Influencing with Integrity*, she says, "The environment—the room, table, chairs, lighting, temperature, and so forth—is also important for the success of the meeting. You should be able to decide the optimum environment for what you want to attain."

One technique for creating a pleasant atmosphere is to use effective lighting. Warm, soft, pastel light bulbs cast a flattering glow. Firelight attracts people to the flickering flames and relaxes and soothes the brain. Spotlights are useful for drawing attention to something particularly important or aesthetic. And dimness has always been a "stimulant" for dancing. Every year my sorority has a Valentine Ball in a very romantic room at a large hotel. Although soothing shades of peach and pale green in a cabbage-rose motif dominate the room, most people do not commence dancing to the live band until the lights are dimmed.

Clever touches and flowers are wonderful ways to enhance your home or party area. Think of how you can convey an atmosphere according to your budget, the theme of the party, and the size of the location. Suggestions for themes are in Chapter 10.

Placement of furniture is important. If you could relate to my sixth-grade dance class story, you will agree that a large room lined with chairs can be a frightening place. Instead, opt for arrangements that will make people comfortable enough to "mix." Try several card tables, covered attractively (or left plain for heavy-duty games), set in an S-configuration. Perhaps a love seat across from a comfortable wing chair and small end table would make a good conversation area for small functions.

The furniture arrangements should be contrived to look as if they are natural areas for easy talking. If you are planning a large party, consider moving the furniture to the perimeter of the room and inviting guests to sit on pillows or rugs on the floor. This can be a delightful atmosphere for a Japanese-style dinner or to mimic a picnic or a day at the beach (see Chapter 10). Of course, you wouldn't expect older guests or people dressed for an elegant dinner to sit on the floor.

In decorating for a party, bear in mind safety, fun, and ease. For example, if you are having a sit-down dinner, don't make your centerpiece so large or imposing that it interferes with the guests' conversation or view of each other. And use candles with caution. If they cannot be monitored throughout the evening, avoid them or use them selectively—when eating. Then blow them out.

Speaking of candles, I must relate a story about a New Year's Eve party I attended at a world-famous hotel. The decorations were all done in sparkling shades of silver contrasting with black and white. The table centerpieces consisted of a mirrored box, supporting a silver candelabra, with silver-sprayed flowers and foliage arranged around the base of the tall black candles. The effect was black-tie dramatic. A single rose and party favors made the tables look festive. But there was one major flaw: When the air-conditioning in the ballroom came on, it blew the candle wicks, and before we knew it, the centerpieces all over the room were in flame!

The fires were quickly put out, but after that experience I always made it a point to consider the safety factor as well as aesthetics in decorating for a party.

It's always a good idea to clear areas of needless clutter or knickknacks before a party. Why take the chance of something getting broken or knocked down? Instead, place these items, arranged in groups, on top of an armoire or shelf, protected from traffic. If you are left with gaps, you could fill them in with real leaves or blossoming branches. Another option is to tie large bundles of flowering dogwood together and display them in a florist's bucket with a raffia bow.

Arranging fall foliage in different golds, reds, and yellows along a banquet table makes an attractive centerpiece. And you can use hollowed-out fruit or vegetables for dips. I've used apples for candle holders, a pumpernickel bread round hollowed out for a pâté, and fat red and green peppers for sauces.

Scents can also be used to enhance a party. Just make sure that the scent is not so overpowering that your guests cannot taste their food. A couple of suggestions for sweet aromas are studding an orange or tangerine with cloves and brewing a potpourri in a simmering pot on the stove. One of my favorite scents in the fall is a simmering pot of apple cider, enhanced with spices and rum. I start with a gallon of apple juice, toss in spices like cloves and cinnamon sticks, and then add a pint of cranberry juice and a cup of rum. It serves a crowd, and also serves to warm my friends, making them chatty and relaxed.

For decorating a tabletop, a shawl looks great, and you can

even use bed sheets. Today's sheets are so varied in design that they can communicate almost any period or look. You can coordinate the room by making slipcovers for furniture or card-table chairs. You don't need to know how to sew to make slipcovers; just gather the fabric at the legs of the chair or couch, and tie it secure with a ribbon or sash. After the party, the sheets are thrown into the washer and dryer, and can go back onto the beds!

A festive treatment for Christmas or any other gift-giving time is to gift-wrap the table. Simply cover the tabletop with shelf paper, tape it underneath, and tie it with a huge ribbon. For individual place mats, you can wrap a thin Styrofoam block with shelf paper and tie it as a package too. If you have the rubber stamps discussed in Chapter 1, you can decorate the shelf paper first.

At a dinner party you can take Polaroid photos of your guests and insert the pictures into small acrylic frames to use as place cards. Guests can take them home as favors.

Speaking of acrylic, there are terrific tableware items fashioned from acrylic. Instead of using expensive glass or crystal, try the acrylic champagne glasses and punch bowls. There is a lot less threat of breakage and they are reusable as well.

For large events, here are some additional suggestions: If the weather is inclement or if your party is scheduled during the winter or rainy season, have a designated area for boots, umbrellas, scarves, and the like. You might think about renting a coatrack so that guests won't have to hunt through mounds of clothing to find their own things. Rental stores generally stock any party item you can think of, such as punch bowls, silver, chairs, wedding arches, skirts for tables, dollies for heavy equipment, and tanks for filling balloons.

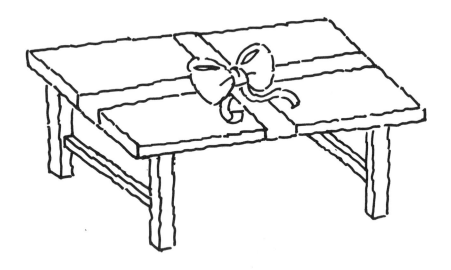

Rolling carts and trays are especially useful for extending a table, serving beverages, and holding tools or buffet ware. A vinyl-covered wire cart can be used to clear away dirty dishes to be washed later. Of course, the services of a caterer or a bartender can provide a lot of ease when you are entertaining large groups. If your budget is thinning, hiring students to help out is another alternative. But no matter who you hire, remember to make sure to give explicit instructions and directions.

Define the traffic flow clearly so that people don't step into each other. It's also a good idea to have two ice buckets (keep ice in good supply), two serving trays, two sets of silverware, and two serving lines set up at opposite ends of the table for efficiency. It's best to set up the beverage-and-drink station away from the food lines.

People are becoming more and more accustomed to potluck

affairs nowadays, with time becoming such a scarce commodity. Don't feel intimidated or bashful about asking people to bring a covered dish, dessert, or drinks for a party. Most people will be more than happy to help out.

Here are a few last-minute reminders: Don't forget to lower the thermostat, leave out lots of napkins and ashtrays, and perk and serve a big pot of coffee so that guests will arrive home safely.

3

LEADERSHIP QUALITIES & TECHNIQUES

Although the ability to lead and inspire others is basically instinctual and acquired through experiences of everyday life, it is something that can be learned as well. This chapter contains specific techniques for leading games at parties. If you follow these techniques as well as your own instincts, and you plan your games sufficiently ahead of time, you will be bound to have a successful games party!

SIX TECHNIQUES FOR EFFECTIVE LEADERSHIP

(1) **Visibility:** The first tip for being an effective games leader has to do with position. The leader must make sure that he or she will be seen and heard. The most logical position then would be at the "head of the class," standing in front of the players. I remember one large party I gave at our community's lake pavilion. Although we were sitting at picnic tables under a protective canopy, when it came time to give directions, I was competing to be heard with bird song, boaters, and other picnickers. To compensate for what was basically open-air acoustics, the best position for me to be heard and seen turned out to be *on* a picnic bench at the head of the pavilion.

For a game player, nothing is more frustrating than to be fired up and ready for action, and then not to be able to hear the instructions. The guests will begin to whisper among themselves, "What did she say?" or "Did you hear that?", and not only will they disturb each other, but they will lose their own interest and motivation.

(2) Signal for attention: After you have the players' attention by being very visible, you must get them to quiet down. To do this, it's best to use a signal of some sort or perhaps two signals. If you are in a location with a piano, chords can be played for attention. In an outdoor setting, a short toot on a whistle can be effective, as long as you don't act like a drill sergeant. No one likes the feeling of being regimented at a party.

Perhaps you are outdoors but in a pavilion area such as the one described earlier. A whistle would have been abrasive; a simple raising of an arm to get attention is enough of a signal. People will usually want to get on with the game, so an overly dramatic signal is not needed or desirable. Remember, you want to get their attention for instructions, but you also want to keep the relaxed atmosphere of the party.

(3) Wait for quiet: You need to wait very patiently for the room to quiet down. If you become anxious and forge ahead, you will find yourself stopping and repeating directions, or worse yet, reprimanding inattentive individuals. This, of course, will dampen everyone's enthusiasm.

(4) Give concise instructions: When you have your audience's attention, make a brief introduction, followed by the instructions for the game. Speak in short, concise, direct sentences.

(5) Know your material and be friendly: Since you will be familiar with the games (you will have chosen them with specific ideas in mind), your directions can be given in a friendly way, with a smile. A leader who is not well acquainted with the material—perhaps reading the instructions for the first time or mispronouncing words—will lose the audience. Also, the leader should refrain from approaching the microphone or the head of the room to tell jokes or otherwise attract attention to him- or herself. The desired effect is to give such succinct—yet friendly—directions that you motivate the players with a minimum of delay or distraction.

(6) Questions: Ask if there are any questions after you have described the objective of the game. It helps to state the object of the game first in two different short versions. You will find that by doing this, you will have no puzzled looks and few questions.

ASSESSING THE PROGRESS OF THE GAME

As the host or games leader, you will hardly ever take part in the games themselves. But you probably won't mind this at all, because you will be in the unique position of being able to watch all the others in action, and to assess the interactive success of the game. Once the game is in gear, and provided that it is fairly long, you can circulate among the players. This way, you can keep track of what's happening and, more importantly, of what's coming next. As a result, you will be ready to give further instructions or introduce the next game. The idea here is to move from one planned activity to another, smoothly. Balance and timing are essential.

To be an effective games leader, don't allow too much time to elapse between games and try to discourage a jumble of activity or inattentiveness. Don't ignore a team's or individual's victory or winning. Don't permit a game to continue on so long that the participants are gazing about bored. Also, try to avoid having your guests standing about between games wondering what they should be doing, while you are reorganizing games or moving furniture.

TIMING
• •

Now that you know about what to avoid, let's analyze how to get the results we do want by taking a closer look at timing. Here are some timing tips to consider:

- Once the action of a game is under way, you may use the time to think about how you are going to word directions to get people into their next formation quickly, and with a minimum of confusion.
- In a contest or relay situation, make sure that you have told the players what the stopping signal will be. With a relay, there should be definite and clear starting and stopping points. With a contest, state a goal or a score of points to be reached that will be a signal to end the game or round of play.
- To make the shift from one game to another easier, plan activities with either the same formation or use a pairing or grouping method to lead into the next game. (See games for forming partners, groups, and teams in Chapter 8.)
- For games involving a predetermined playing time, say 5 or 10 minutes of play, use a kitchen timer for accuracy. I suggest that you also begin the game with a loud command, such as "Ready? Set? Go!" Tell the players ahead of time what the start command will be, and then you can say, "When the timer sounds at the end of 10 minutes, the round is over. Stop what you're doing (counting, searching, or whatever) and sit down where you are." Or you can say, "When I stop the music (or blow the whistle or ring the bell), count your beans (or the contest score) and get into a tight circle." Ideally, the next round or the next game should be set up around the formation of a circle.

When the game is over, allow enough time for the winning team or person to enjoy the victory. Then call or signal for attention, wait until you've gotten it, and begin again.

Occasionally, you will come across a game where there is only a suggested time of play and you may wonder how you will know when to stop. The exact point will be difficult to determine and experience with the game will be your best guide. However, if you are new to leadership in games, you will need to keep a finely tuned ear and a sharp eye on the group's progress to estimate its degree of exhilaration. It's best to stop while players are still a

little keyed up and having a good time; this way, you can channel their enthusiasm into the next game. With that said, for leaders with little experience, here are some timing suggestions.

- **Pre-party games:** It's nice when all the guests arrive on time, but I find that this rarely happens. So it's a good idea to start a pre-party game after about two thirds of the people have arrived. Then let the activity continue on for another 10 minutes to include as many guests as possible.
- **Hunts and collecting:** If competitors are collecting notes or other items, try to allow for about eight transactions or turns. However, I have had to adjust this number in the

past, when I discovered that the contestants were so clever that several of them were reaching the same goal rather quickly.

- **Games with *"It"* or a leader:** If the group is taking turns being either the leader or *It,* four or five changes in leadership or *It* are about right. Groups of about five couples, or pairs, with five changes in leadership, lend themselves to a well-paced activity length. It seems that with anything larger, the people in the team get tired of waiting for their turn.
- **Mixers:** Getting-acquainted games, sometimes called "mixers," "icebreakers," or "defrosters," work best for a duration of 3 to 5 minutes. If the group is comprised of total strangers, the game can be longer.

Most of the games that I have conducted over the years either have a goal or a tangible means of timing. If not, I always try to recommend a length of time or watch for a group reaction. By all means, if a game is obviously failing, take the initiative to stop it and go on with something else.

In *Managing,* a book on leadership in management, Harold Geneen says, "One of the essential attributes of a good leader is enough self-confidence to be able to admit his own mistakes and know that they won't ruin him. The true test is to be able to recognize what is wrong as early as possible and then to set about rectifying the situation."

FORMATIONS

You should have no trouble getting people into groups or various formations like a circle or line. The group will be looking to you for directions. However, if you have an assistant, forming a circle, for example, is best accomplished with the assistant, as part of the group, saying, "Let's hold hands and get into a circle." More about assistants follows.

THE USE OF ASSISTANTS

Assistants are valuable for a games leader because they can assume a variety of duties to help alleviate some of the concerns of the leader. And for the guests, they can boost enthusiasm and increase confidence in the games. A wise host or leader will treat assistants with respect and appreciation.

Before a game begins, the assistants should be introduced to the whole group. It is possible that a game or skill will require a "walk-through," and if your helpers are identified ahead of time, players will know whom to seek out for assistance.

For large events, try to have enough helpers so that they can switch off and everyone can participate at some time or other in the games. Do not exhaust them.

Often assistants can be called upon to act as a judge. Their unique position gives them some authority and the game players will welcome their unbiased opinion—unbiased because they are not actually taking part in the competition. Sometimes the games leader will be preparing supplies or setting up the next series of games, and assistants can be available to oversee the progress of the ongoing game.

Go over the party's program in advance with your helpers to establish an order of events and to anticipate any glitches. Identify their specific duties and show them the equipment to be handed out, how chairs or formations are to be used, and where the prizes are to be stowed away. This preplanning will help your assistants help you set the tone and pace of the party and will increase your helpers' effectiveness. Here are some duties that assistants can perform:

- greet guests or answer the door or telephone
- take coats or wraps
- hand out and fill in name tags
- distribute supplies for games
- direct people into groups
- fill in for an odd number or for a partner in a game
- even up teams
- help people into a particular formation such as a circle or line
- set up equipment or chairs for the next game
- serve as a judge or time keeper
- dispose of materials and move equipment when a game is over
- change the music
- serve as a demonstrator of a task or as an example
- motivate and encourage guests
- set up and serve refreshments
- lend a hand for cleanup

Actually, cleaning up can be fun with a few helpers hanging around after a party. Play music to make the work move faster, have cleaning supplies on hand, and when you're done, have another cup of coffee, another slice of pie, and relax. It's time to take satisfaction in a job well done.

CONGENIAL COMPANY

Good behavior and appropriate conduct do not apply solely to the host. Here are a few ideas on how to be a good guest, someone whom people will want to invite back to parties over and over.

- Before you assume it's all right to bring another guest to a party, call and ask for your host's or hostess's permission. This simple consideration is especially helpful in the planning of games where numbers make a difference, and perhaps you can contribute to the refreshments for the favor.
- Take it upon yourself to help keep the party rolling by mingling among the other guests. It wouldn't hurt to do

some advance "research" on who will be there and to be able to converse with them straight out.

- Help out in a quiet manner. If you notice that an item needs replenishing and you are quite familiar with the house and host, simply add more ice to the bucket or bring out more cheese wedges, for example. A busy host will appreciate this.
- Don't make an obvious entrance or exit. If you either arrive late or have to leave early, do it as unobtrusively as possible so as not to interrupt the flow of the party.
- Bring a token of friendship or a small gift for your host. A bottle of wine or a bouquet of flowers will always be appreciated.
- Wear a watch and don't overstay your welcome.

4
MOTIVATING YOUR GUESTS

Motivating your guests starts well in advance of your party. The invitations, created with the party theme in mind and designed with a bit of ingenuity or imagination, are your first steps in promoting enthusiasm for your party. For a large community event, in addition to the invitations, the use of newspaper articles and advertisements along with posters and a clever skit serve to create an interested public. Don't underestimate the effect of "word of mouth." Getting people talking about your upcoming event is sure to emphasize its importance. Suggest that the party planners mention the party often in their daily dealings with others. The more people talk about the party, the greater will be their enthusiasm and attendance.

Whether you are hosting a public event or a smaller private party, the way that you welcome someone into your home or party area is extremely important in getting things off to a proper start. I love it when my host is readied at the door, waiting to collect my coat and usher me to a seat or the beverage cart. It projects a feeling of *"Mi casa es su casa"* ("My house is your house") and makes me feel comfortable immediately. If you find that you are busy with other duties or last-minute food preparations or instructions, greeting guests is one of the duties that can be given over to an assistant. My children are often the first to answer the door to welcome my friends and tell them to "Come on in." As the host or hostess, you have the option of prearranging who the first guest will be to arrive. This guest should be someone who is outgoing and has a contagious laugh. He or she would also be a good person to answer the door or greet new arrivals at the beverage cart.

Of course, the atmosphere you create as well as the theme and

games you choose will have a great effect on your guests' motivation.

One of my favorite games is called What's New? It's a pre-party game. The reason I like it so much is that it gives me a chance to greet each guest individually. I take each player to a separate room, away from the others, and pin an object on his or her clothes. Everyone is given a list of the objects to be found and instructed to search for them on each other. While I am safety-pinning some small token onto their clothes, we can talk for a few minutes and I can infect them with the party spirit. I am excited about the party, the people, and I project this attitude. (Precise instructions for this game are given in Chapter 5.)

For quick motivation, get right into the games. Don't let people group themselves off in small, exclusive circles. Once you have introduced the first game, let the group's response play itself out for a few minutes. Enjoy yourself and the wry comments and jokes that your friends will make. This personal contact, made with a smile and a chuckle, will make everyone feel comfortable and relaxed.

Everyone wants to be a winner. Everyone wants to be with a winner. Let everyone at your party feel like a winner sometime throughout the party.

Don't ever let someone be singled out as a bad example of game playing. Parties should provide friendship and a sense of belonging. They are times when we can learn more about ourselves through interaction with others.

There are certain types of television shows that my husband will not watch. He calls them "entertainment by embarrassment." They usually involve a situation where people are laughing at others. These shows seem to be based on hurting someone's self-esteem or dignity for the sake of a laugh. Entertainment by embarrassment. Don't let anyone become the butt of a joke. Many psychological games are constructed to reveal hidden or unexpected views or perhaps the darker side of relationships. It's best not to overdo the power of these games by poking fun at people or addressing their shortcomings or fears.

Cheating or rule dodging should also be avoided. They spoil the fun for everyone and create a negative mood. Utmost attention should be paid to not letting games get rough. You also need to watch that you don't conduct games too quickly. Rushed activities often leave people feeling tired, harassed, and hot.

I remember one game (Steal-a-Gift in Chapter 6) where I did not anticipate any problems. The game involved rolling dice and winning small prizes. There were teams of five players at each table. In the middle of the table were five wrapped prizes (fun items, but nothing of great value, like key rings and hair barrettes). One person starts the roll of the dice. The players get one roll at a time. If they throw a 7 or 11, they take one gift from the pile in the middle. When these gifts are all gone, they may go to another table and steal a gift. If they roll a double 1 (snake eyes) or a double 6 (boxcars), they must return a gift, if they have one. Well, I underestimated the competitiveness and energy of the teenagers in the group, some of whom would not give up a gift—and were rolling on the floor trying to keep them. A few others ran to their cars to put the items out of reach! The other adults and I just stood there with our mouths open, watching the ruckus, and only after all the gifts were snatched back and put away were we able to restore order. You want people to get into the spirit of the game but not to the extent that they feel that anything goes. From now on, we won't play that game with teenagers. Understanding the maturity level of guests and then choosing appropriate games was the lesson learned that day.

Some of your guests may need encouragement to participate. Not everyone is a doer, however. These people can act as motivators for others by giving support and encouragement from the sidelines. They can be cheerleaders. I would never force anyone to play. But with some people all it takes to get them to join in is a confident partner or a "walk-through" or a demonstration of the game. Extend sincere appreciation to your guests for their efforts, especially if they are newcomers or are unfamiliar with the surroundings or with the other guests. By encouraging and congratulating them, you boost their morale and let them know that they can do it if they try.

As already discussed in Chapter 2, timing is everything when it comes to game-playing parties. Your advance planning will make all the difference in the flow of activities and in how relaxed and confident you will be as a leader. The overall games program for a party will probably not last more than an hour, or an hour and a half at most. Of course, the games are interspersed with other activities, like eating, talking, singing, and dancing, so they go into making up an entire afternoon or evening of fun.

You should have more activities or games planned than you will be able to use. That way, if something goes wrong or doesn't turn out as planned, you can move quickly into another game and not lose the enthusiasm you have worked so hard to build up. The important thing is to be flexible.

At organized games parties your first intention should be to get people moving. The games that do this best are the pre-party games, which make people touch, talk, and move around each other. Pre-party games also provide some additional time for latecomers to arrive and still join in without feeling noticeably late.

Pre-party games are followed by "get-acquainted" games, also called "icebreakers" and "defrosters." These types of games address everyone together as a group and usually involve a simple task that makes people interact with each other. They are lively and fast-paced and let people loosen up and meet each other. Icebreakers are interesting to observe from a distance because a transformation takes place. People with entirely different personalities or of different backgrounds are brought together, and at the end of the game, you often see them patting each other on the back, sometimes hugging, and genuinely happy to have met one another.

Changing the pace of the games is a good way to keep up your guests' motivation. For example, if you have just had twenty people run a relay, they will need time to cool down, get a drink, and relax. After that, it would be a good time for a pencil-and-paper game or contest. If you have a stunt or a skit to perform, this would also be the ideal time for it.

Throughout the games program, vary the games so that people change partners often, sometimes play alone, and mix around. But try to bring the whole group back together for the last game. For example, save an icebreaker or relay for last, just before the refreshments are served. It will leave the group feeling whole and connected from having "lived through" the last activity together. Be sure to let the group know that this is the last game and what will be coming next, such as refreshments.

For large functions, one master of ceremonies is all that's needed. As with too many cooks, too many leaders are not advisable, and can diffuse the guests' motivation. Assistants or helpers at a large function should know what's expected of them so as not to interfere but to know when and where to be available.

All the essential equipment, such as the microphones, piano, and curtains need to be readied and in good working condition. If people are forced to wait because of a dead microphone, for example, you will often lose their interest and motivation.

Your party area should be well-ventilated and, if necessary, air-conditioned. Lots of warm bodies can account for quite a bit of heat in a room, and with a large group of active game players, I would lower the temperature even more. If your guests are hot and pooped out, they won't have much motivation.

In addition to your scheduled games, it's always a good idea to have other supplies and games available. When packing for a picnic or outdoor party, for instance, you might include a Frisbee, a baseball and bat, a croquet set, a volleyball and net, and a badminton set. After you have played a series of icebreaker games and finished your lunch would be a good time to set this equipment out on a table. Generally, someone will get a game going and the others can relax with their drinks.

When we had our hayride (described in Chapter 2), as I was gazing into the evening bonfire, it occurred to me that I should

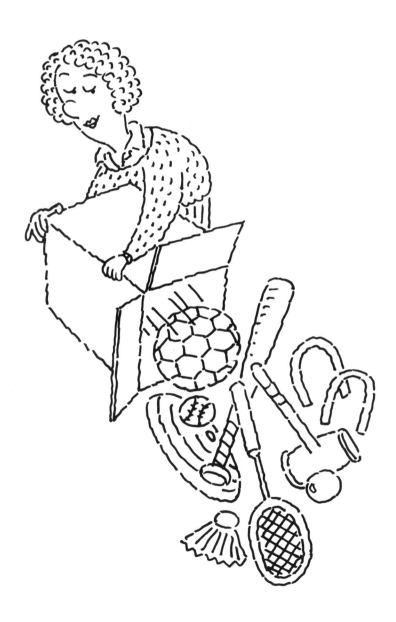

have brought a guitar. With everyone exhilarated from the chilly ride and huddled together drinking hot chocolate in front of the fire, the scene would have been complete with some group singing to the strumming of a guitar.

For indoor gatherings, put out "solo" games such as puzzles (start a corner so that it will scream "finish me"). For interactive fun without instructions, put out stacks of playing cards, pick-up sticks, Chinese checkers, and Backgammon.

For a family reunion at Christmastime, all you need to do to get people motivated for a "work party" is to set out lots of thread or flossing string, cranberries, and popcorn. Family members can create string decorations over chatter and coffee. Work parties are fun for those who enjoy cooking and handiwork. Set out cookie cutters and dough, corn for husking, peas for shelling, nuts for cracking, and for the industrious, pulpwood or soap for carving.

The theme of a party can also be a great motivator. My sorority once had a party with a Monte Carlo theme. We found someone who was well versed in gambling games, like Craps, Roulette, 21, and a type of Keno, who attended one of our organizational meetings and taught us how to be dealers. We obtained the equipment through Rotary Club connections. We dressed in costume to look ·like dealers, and made arrangements for concessions so that we could have kegs of beer and cases of soft drinks, and we sold nachos and popcorn. We even had a separate area for Bingo. As it turned out, this was one of the most profitable events we ever had, as well as one of the most entertaining. Even though there is no direct leadership with this type of party, people will mill around, watch the games, and take a chance.

Getting people to form partners is really no problem at a games party. If your guests arrive as couples, of course, there is no need to worry about who will work with whom. But if your group consists of "singles" or of people who don't know each other, then a device for forming partners is sometimes needed.

One of the best ways to do this is through the use of name tags. On one tag paste a character from the frame of a comic strip, and on another tag paste a character from the frame that follows. If you were using "Peanuts," for example, have the two people find each other by matching, say, Charlie Brown and Linus.

In addition to comic-strip characters, people can match themselves with the following:

- puzzle pieces
- colors
- shapes
- proverbs
- song lyrics
- famous couples

You can use all kinds of ideas and concepts for matching name tags. Try to think of something to coordinate with your theme.

Another way of forming partners is to have guests draw an item out of a bag, and when everyone has his or her pick, the matching begins. For instance, you could cut swatches of plaid fabrics in half and two people can match them up. This is a great theme gimmick for a Clan Party—matching tartans. Then you can use the names of the plaid clans to match people up for their dinner seating arrangements: The McIntoshs sit there, the McDermotts here, on place cards.

It's best to plan your partner matching for as early as possible. Having a partner makes people feel more comfortable and able to participate more easily, whereas being a loner at a party can be tough. Also, the pre-party activities are more fun when two people work together.

Verbal instructions, like "Take someone's hands," "Form a circle," and "Back to back," are alternate ways of forming partners, but random matching tricks are more like games themselves and tend to be less awkward. After all, the most important reason for forming partners is for your guests to feel comfortable and secure. For specific "games" for forming partners, groups, and teams, turn to Chapter 8.

5
PRE-PARTY GAMES, CONTESTS & ICEBREAKERS

Chapters 5 through 8 contain more than a hundred games for you to choose from for your next game-playing party or event. I suggest that you make a small investment of a recipe box and a few packages of 4" x 6" ruled index cards. As you work your way through these chapters, find games that appeal to you and are appropriate for different functions, and then write them out on your own cards, creating a personal game file. Put the instructions for the game on one side of the card, and the equipment or supplies needed on the other. Save some space on the bottom of the card for personal notes—tips that you have discovered that will help you in the future. By adapting the games in various ways, you will learn what works best for you and your guests.

Invite new people to your parties. Their unfamiliar presence will add new life and dimension. Juggle your guest list. There's no better way to meet and bond with new people than to share your old friends with newcomers at a games party.

PRE-PARTY GAMES

Pre-party games accomplish several purposes. Most importantly, they help to establish the tone and mood for the rest of the party. They also allow time for guests to arrive, give your present guests something to do, can be played in a short time span, and keep your guests from feeling that they have to wait around for the party to begin. Without further introduction then, begin.

Name of the game: In the Bag.   **# of players:** Any.
Type: Pre-party.
Supplies: Ten lunch-type paper bags, with one article in each bag. Close and number the bags. Pencils and paper.
Formation: Guests circulate.
Object of the game: To guess what is in the bags.
Play action: As guests arrive, they are given paper and pencil. They circulate around, feeling the different bags, and then write their guesses as to what the bags contain.
Hints and tips: Advise people to be gentle with the bags, since pressing too hard will break them open. About 20 minutes is a good length of time for this game. When the time is up, the leader opens the bags and reveals the items. The winner is the one with the most correct answers.
Adaptation: Put objects in the bags to coordinate with the theme of the party. For example, at a baby shower the bags could contain a diaper, huge safety pin, washcloth, bib, bottle, pacifier, hairbrush, teething item, thermometer, and baby powder.

Name of the game: First Impression.   **# of players:** Any.
Type: Pre-party and get-acquainted.
Supplies: Cards, pencils, and pins or transparent tape.
Formation: Guests circulate, with a card pinned or taped on their back.
Object of the game: To meet others.
Play action: As guests circulate, they write a short description or first impression of each other on the card on each others' back.
Hints and tips: The leader should provide sample descriptions, like "hot stuff" or "literary genius"—nothing too literal. The fun is in exaggerated or elaborate descriptions, but they shouldn't be insulting or embarrassing. After 10 minutes or so, the group is called together, and the players read their neighbor's card.

Name of the game: Finders Meeters.   **# of players:** 20 or more.
Type: Pre-party and get-acquainted.
Supplies: Cards prepared by the host in advance and pencils.
Formation: Guests circulate.
Object of the game: To get better acquainted.
Play action: Guests circulate, talking with others, in order to fill in the items on the cards. Allow 10 or 15 minutes for this game as guests are arriving. The leader announces the person with

the most names on his or her list. This person then introduces the people on his or her list.

Hints and tips: The card list is made up by the leader and should contain interests or hobbies of the guests. Examples:

1. Knows someone in politics—Name: _____
   Who: _____
2. Carries a good luck item—Name: _____
   What: _____
3. Travelled out of the country—Name: _____
   Where: _____
4. Plays a musical instrument—Name: _____
   Instrument: _____
5. Owns a foreign-model car—Name: _____
   Model: _____
6. Works a garden—Name: _____
7. Has had a different/strange experience—Name: _____
   What: _____
8. Has an unusual collection—Name: _____
   Articles: _____
9. Has been on TV and/or in a movie—Name: _____
   What: _____
10. Lives the farthest away—Name: _____
    Where: _____

Name of the game: Mystery Guest. **# of players:** 20 or more.
Type: Pre-party and get-acquainted.
Supplies: Paper and pencil. Prize.
Formation: Guests circulate.
Object of the game: To become better acquainted.
Play action: As people get acquainted, they are to try to find out as much about each other as possible, taking notes. At the end of the party, the leader reads a list of facts about the mystery guest. As soon as anyone recognizes who the mystery guest is, he or she shouts out the name and wins a prize.
Hints and tips: Mystery-guest information suggestions:

1. Where he or she grew up and went to school
2. Hobbies
3. Special interests or collections
4. Favorite foods
5. Favorite colors
6. Pets
7. Latest or farthest travels
8. Job or occupation
9. Family interests
10. Spouse's job

Name of the game: What's New?   **# of players:** 12–30.
Type: Pre-party.
Supplies: Paper or index cards with items to be found. Ten to twelve small objects that can be hidden on guests. Transparent tape or safety pins to attach items. Pencils.
Formation: Guests circulate, examining others.
Object of the game: To find the hidden items on the card list, and write the guest's name beside each item as it is discovered.
Play action: As guests arrive, the leader calls them individually to another room, where a small object is pinned or taped to their person. Everyone is then given a list of the objects to be found and instructed to search for them among the guests.
Hints and tips: The objects should be in a place where they are visible yet difficult to see right away. Hide items on socks, almost under collars, on cuffs of pants, in patterned fabric, at belt buckles, in hair. . . . This is fun because it gets people moving around and looking at each other. Try 5 minutes or less if your guests are observant. Sample list of items:

1. jingle bell
2. key
3. rose
4. button
5. clothespin
6. colored bead
7. diaper pin
8. Boy Scout badge
9. clothes label
10. peppermint pipe cleaner
11. holly berries
12. miniature plastic dinosaur
13. miniature toy car
14. miniature cowboy boot
15. feather

Name of the game: String Along.   **# of players:** 10 or more.
Type: Pre-party (in partners).
Supplies: Anywhere from 50 to 300 pieces of string cut in different lengths from 4 to 36". The strings are hidden throughout the room or house ahead of time.
Formation: Guests hunt.
Object of the game: To collect string as partners.
Play action: On a signal, partners find and collect pieces of string, tying them together in connected lengths as they go. The couple with the longest continuous length of string wins.
Hints and tips: Limit this activity to about 3 to 4 minutes. It is not necessary to find all of the hidden string.
Adaptation: A special colored string, if found and tied in, earns a

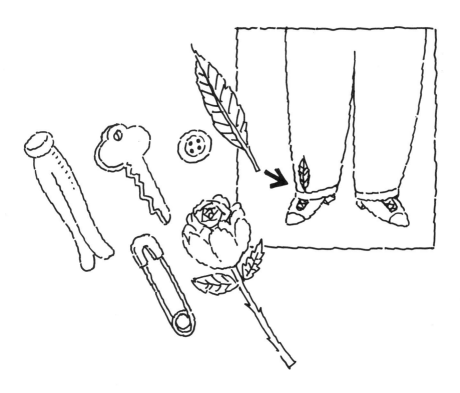

special prize, or the couple with it starts the next game or does a stunt, etc. This game can be adapted at Christmastime or for a birthday party using ribbon. As another option, the longest length of one color tied together nets a prize.

Name of the game: Bean Dealer.   **# of players:** 10 or more.
Type: Pre-party and get-acquainted.
Supplies: Envelopes with the same number of beans—15 to 20 in each.
Formation: Guests circulate and barter.
Object of the game: Each guest is given an envelope and instructed to circulate and collect the most beans possible.
Play action: The players approach one guest at a time to guess the number of beans in his or her closed fist. They address the person and ask, "Odd or even?" Once they are told and if they guess correctly, they get to take the beans. If they guess incorrectly, they must give away that number of beans.
Hints and tips: Allow less than 10 minutes.

In addition to these games, you might leave a conversation piece out for arriving guests to have something to look at or discuss. I have a collection of old-style wooden toys that invite people to "try them out."

If your group is a creative bunch, supply early arrivals with paper or cloth bibs as well as such items as yarn, jewels, buttons, pom-poms, markers, scissors, and glue, so that they can design their own bibs. This gives guests something to do and creates a climate for easy conversation.

You can also let guests decorate a banana. They can use a soft-tipped pen to draw the features and make hats or clothes out of construction paper. Award a prize for the best banana, take photos of the participants with their creations, and then invite everyone to select ice cream and toppings for (what else?) banana splits!

PRE-PARTY CONTESTS
· ·

Pre-party contests are similar to pre-party games in that they eliminate awkwardness by giving your guests something to do immediately on their arrival. Contests also serve to loosen up the atmosphere—almost everyone likes to play guessing games. In addition, you can create a "carnival" feeling by setting up several different displays. And since these contests are mostly self-explanatory, they free you up to greet people, hang coats, and show new guests around.

Name of the game: Guess the Weight.   **# of players:** Small group.
Type: Pre-party contest.
Supplies: Tray of articles that have been weighed and numbered. Paper and pencil for each player. Prize(s).
Formation: Casual mixing.
Object of the game: To guess the weight of the items.
Play action: Players may lift the articles; then they write down their estimate of their weight. The player with the closest estimates gets a prize.
Adaptation: Follow the same type of idea, but the object here is to guess lengths. Use a ball of string, roll of tape, skein of yarn, spool of thread, reel of wire, yards of cloth, etc.

Name of the game: Guess How Many.   **# of players:** Small group.
Type: Pre-party contest.
Supplies: Books and newspaper. Paper and pencils. Prize(s).
Formation: Casual mixing.
Object of the game: To guess correctly or come closest.
Play action: The books may be picked up but *must remain closed,* as the competitors try to guess the number of pages. With the newspaper, they are to guess the number of words in preselected columns. Players log their guesses on paper.

Name of the game: How Many, How Much?   **# of players:**
Small to medium-sized group.
Type: Pre-party contest.
Supplies: Cards and pencils for each player. In addition to the
prize, the following items are on the table:

1. Straight pins stuck in a cushion
2. A heap of matches or pennies
3. A dish of navy beans
4. A clear jar of crackers
5. A roll of ribbon
6. A skein of wool (rolled into a ball)
7. A sheet of paper with intersecting circles drawn on it
8. A clear box of party toothpicks

Formation: Guests look at the items spread out on the table, but
do not touch.
Object of the game: Competitors guess the numbers and quantities, and write down their answers on paper numbered 1 through 8 or whatever.
Play action: When the number or quantity of the items is called out, players must note the extent to which they are off each time. For example, if someone guessed 290 navy beans and there were 298 on the table, they would jot down 8. The person with the lowest total number is the winner.
Hints and tips: Cards and directions can be left on the table for indirect instruction.

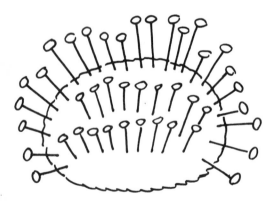

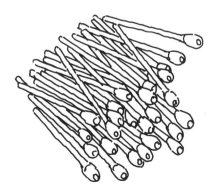

Name of the game: Signs and Signals. **# of players:** Small group.

Type: Pre-party contest.

Supplies: Prepared individual lists or one poster with the list. Paper and pencil.

Formation: Guests either mingling or seated in teams.

Object of the game: To figure out the signs or signals in 5 minutes.

Play action: Players fill in the stars to complete the command.

1. K***L***
2. N*E***
3. B*****O*D**
4. N*P******
5. L***T*O***
6. K***O**T**G****
7. N*R****T***
8. N*S******

9. R********
10. C******
11. M**W******
12. O**W**
13. B**S***
14. Y****R****O*W**
15. D***W***

Answers:

1. Keep Left
2. No Exit
3. Beware of Dog
4. No Parking
5. Lift to Open
6. Keep Off the Grass
7. No Right Turn
8. No Smoking

9. Restrooms
10. Caution
11. Men Working
12. One Way
13. Bus Stop
14. Yield Right of Way
15. Don't Walk

Name of the game: Wool Ravel. **# of players:** Small group.

Type: Pre-party contest.

Supplies: Ball or skein of wool. Wool wound in and out the legs and backs of chairs. Prize(s).

Formation: Players are seated on their chairs.

Object of the game: To quickly untangle the wool without breaking it, and eventually wind it back into a ball.

Play action: Players must remain seated in their chairs while they disentangle the wool strands and roll them back into a ball. The first player finished wins.

Name of the game: Tip the Orange.   **# of players:** Two at a time, with two or three pairs playing simultaneously.
Type: Pre-party contest.
Supplies: Spoons and oranges or tennis balls.
Formation: Two opponents standing.
Object of the game: To knock off your opponent's orange, while keeping your own.
Play action: Both players have a spoon in each hand. The right spoon holds an orange. The goal is to knock off your opponent's orange, but still hold on to your own. Have play-offs.

For pre-party contests where the purpose is to guess the quantity of items in a container, you might have the container and the items relate to your theme. For instance, at a cowboy party, the container could be a boot or a 10-gallon hat, and could hold peanuts in the shell. At a spaghetti supper, you could fill a colander with pasta and macaroni. At Christmastime, you can use small glitter-balls in a glass bowl, which can also double as a decoration. Try silver-wrapped candy kisses on Valentine's Day. The possibilities are endless.

CONTESTS
· ·

These contests can be used at any point during a party.

Name of the game: How Old?   **# of players:** Any.
Type: Contest (individuals or teams).
Supplies: The correct ages of famous people or celebrities written down. Pencil and paper. Prize(s).
Formation: Circle of players sitting.
Object of the game: To guess the ages of the famous.
Play action: To guess the most correctly or the closest. Total up the differences in the ages and the guesses. The winner will be the one with the smallest number.
Hints and tips: I like to read the names out loud because the group's comments add to the fun. I also read the answers out loud and let them check their own papers. But another option is to have the names written out on a large sheet of paper. The ages of famous people and their birthdays appear on the celebrity pages of most newspapers every Sunday. Notices are also in daily papers. Save them for a few weeks. Examples: Nov. 1990: Kurt Vonnegut, 68; Nadia Comaneci, 29; King Hussein, 55; Howard Baker, 65; Lauren Hutton, 47; Prince Charles, 42; Katharine Hepburn, 83; Ted Turner, 52; William F. Buckley, 65; Rodney Dangerfield, 69; Linda Evans, 48. . . .

Name of the game: Where in the World?   **# of players:** Any.
Type: Contest (individuals or teams).
Supplies: Trace the outline of countries or states from a large atlas. Place on colored paper and cut out. Paper and pencil. Prize(s).
Formation: Casual seating with paper and pencil, either as individuals or teams.
Object of the game: To get the most correct answers.
Play action: The leader holds up the cutout countries or states and gives each a number. Or they can be tacked to a bulletin board or wall. Players write their answers on numbered paper.
Adaptation: Pictures of well-known resorts cut out of magazines and numbered. Players guess locations. You can have two categories: continents and countries. Great for travel clubs!

Name of the game: True or False.   **# of players:** Two teams.
Type: Team contest.
Supplies: List of questions prepared ahead of time. Chairs.
Formation: Two teams seated on chairs facing each other. An empty chair is placed at each end, between the two rows of players. They are told that one chair is the "true" chair and the other is the "false" chair.
Object of the game: To secure the correct-answer chair first. Scores one point.
Play action: The leader makes a statement to each pair of players in turn. If they believe it is a true statement, they have to run and sit in the "true chair." If false, they head for the "false chair." Sometimes both will rush for the same chair, but the first seated scores a point for his or her team.
Hints and tips: I derived my questions from the dictionary. Sample questions:

1. Etymology is the study of insects.
2. November has 30 days.
3. Port is the left side of a ship.
4. Rio de Janeiro is in Argentina.
5. Animosity is friendliness.
6. A rhombus is an equilateral parallelogram.
7. A debacle is a deadlock.
8. The word "protocol" has nine letters.
9. A linebacker is a defensive player.
10. Holland is the same as The Netherlands.
11. Hanukkah is a 12-day festival.
12. A fluke is on a whale.
13. The Euphrates flows through Iraq into the Persian Gulf.
14. The word "circa" indicates an approximate date.
15. A sergeant is ranked below a captain and a lieutenant.

Answers:

1. F, words	9. T, behind the line
2. T	10. T
3. T	11. F, 8-day
4. F, Brazil	12. T, the tail
5. F, hatred	13. T
6. T	14. T
7. F, a crushing defeat	15. T
8. F, 8 letters	

Name of the game: Alliteration.   **# of players:** Small group.
Type: Team contest.
Supplies: Small pieces of paper with a letter of the alphabet on each, except for j, k, q, v, x, and z. Score pad for leader. Hat. Timer.
Formation: Two teams sitting comfortably.
Object of the game: To name the most words.
Play action: One player from the first team draws a letter out of the hat. In 30 seconds, the player calls out as many words as he or she can that begin with that letter. A count is tallied. The process is repeated for a member of the other team. The teams alternate until everyone has had a turn.

Name of the game: Men vs. Women.   **# of players:** Two teams.
Type: Contest.
Supplies: List of questions and answers prepared in advance. Fair and unbiased audience for scoring.
Formation: Two teams facing one another.
Object of the game: To make the correct response or the best execution first.
Play action: Pose a question or task to both teams simultaneously for the first correct response. Then pose another, and so on.
Hints and tips: Tailor the contest to your group's interests. Suggestions:

1. Spell "sepulchral."
2. Imitate a monkey.
3. What is the population of Mexico?
4. Name your state's senators.
5. How do you make fettuccine?
6. Where will the next Olympics be held?
7. Imitate a dog or cat fight.
8. Whistle the tune of an Irish song.
9. Name three things that are always yellow.
10. Name one wonder of the Seven Wonders of the Ancient World.
11. Name the branches of the Federal Government.
12. How many bones are in the human body?

ICEBREAKERS

Icebreaker games are sometimes called "defrosters" or "chill chasers" and are often thought to be the same as "get-acquainted" games. But we can make a distinction between icebreaker games and get-acquainted activities, in that icebreakers are set up to encourage intermingling and conviviality, whereas get-acquainted games are primarily designed to help people learn and practise the names of the other guests. Yet there can be some crossover between the two types.

Both of these types of games should be played in a relaxed atmosphere and cause people to think or perform a task together. For the success of both varieties, I stress simple directions so that the effort of the players is expended in playing the game and not in trying to understand the action. Also, do not let any activity drag on too long or become too familiar.

In respect to the get-acquainted games, make sure that the introductions are made correctly. Pronounce people's names slowly and loudly. A good technique is to have each guest introduce another, say, the person on his or her left. When people introduce themselves, they have a tendency to hurry or speak too softly. It's also a delight to hear your own name.

One other note: These activities can be used at any point in the program. Try interspersing them between relays or stunts for a change of pace.

Name of the game: Beautiful Baby.   **# of players:** Any.
Type: Icebreaker.
Supplies: The guests bring a photo of themselves as an infant or young child. Bulletin board for display. Paper and pencils.
Formation: Guests circulate.
Object of the game: To identify the most photos correctly.
Play action: Pin up each photo with a number above it on the bulletin board. Give everyone a piece of paper with as many numbers as there are pictures. As the party progresses, players try to guess which photo corresponds to each guest. At some point, collect all the papers. The winner will be the one who has matched the most pictures with the right people at the party.
Hints and tips: This is best played with people who know each other's names. The prize could be a small photo album, or a photography-related item for a camera club.

Name of the game: What's in a Name?   **# of players:** Any.
Type: Icebreaker.
Supplies: Paper with the name of a famous person written on it. Straight pins or transparent tape.
Formation: Guests circulate.
Object of the game: To guess who you are.
Play action: A famous person's name is pinned on the back of each guest. The guests approach one another, asking questions about themselves. The response can only be a "yes" or a "no." The first person to guess who they are wins a prize.
Hints and tips: The leader can suggest that they ask such questions as "Am I a male?", "Am I a cartoon character?", and so on. Suggestions for names:

- Vincent Van Gogh
- Godzilla
- Princess Di
- Spuds MacKenzie
- Madonna
- Stevie Wonder
- Don Johnson
- Dolly Parton
- Goldie Hawn
- Gandhi
- Marco Polo
- Julio Iglesias
- James Bond (007)
- Superman
- Dracula (Count)
- Winston Churchill
- Bugs Bunny
- Albert Einstein
- Christie Brinkley

- Amadeus
- Bruce Springsteen
- Ernest Hemingway
- Julius Caesar
- Miss Piggy
- Martina Navratilova
- Garfield the Cat
- Captain Spock
- Mikhail Baryshnikov
- Charles Dickens
- Roy Rogers
- Pinocchio
- Napoleon Bonaparte
- Marilyn Monroe
- Pee Wee Herman
- Sherlock Holmes
- Agatha Christie
- Neil Armstrong
- Adolf Hitler

Adaptation: An advertisement is pinned on the back of each player. Conversation is made about the player's product, without actually saying what the product is. From the comments made by the others, each tries to guess the product he or she is advertising. Scan magazines and newspapers for products. Suggestions: a Toyota, hemorrhoid medicine, perfume, a bank, a computer, or clothing such as jeans.

Name of the game: Just Your Name and Number.   **# of players:** Any.

Type: Get-acquainted.

Supplies: Name cards, paper, and pencils. Pins or transparent tape.

Formation: Get-acquainted.

Object of the game: To learn the names of other guests.

Play action: Each member of the party is given a card with a number on it. They are instructed to write their name on the blank side and to wear the card with their name showing. Later in the evening, the leader asks the guests to turn over their name card and expose the number only. Each guest then writes down as many names and numbers as possible.

Name of the game: Couples' Quiz.   **# of players:** Any even number.

Type: Get-acquainted or icebreaker (in couples).

Supplies: Paper and pencil. Planned questions.

Formation: One person in the couple leaves the room.

Object of the game: To learn more about each other.

Play action: The leader tailors some questions to the group and the particular couples. One person in each of the couples leaves the room. The others remain and are asked questions about their partner, spouse, or date. They answer the questions the way they think their partners would respond. Their answers are written down. When the missing partners return, they are asked the same questions but give their own answers. One point is logged for each match. In the next round, the partners' roles are reversed.

Name of the game: Sack Shake.   **# of players:** Any.

Type: Icebreaker.

Supplies: A small brown bag for each player. Soft-tipped pens. Prize.

Formation: Guests circulate.

Object of the game: To get to know each with laughs.

Play action: Each player covers his or her writing hand with a bag and approaches another and asks for an autograph on the bag. The autograph is to be written with the hand usually not used—thus, right-handers sign with their left and vice versa for lefties. The one with the most signatures when "time" is called wins a prize.

Name of the game: Mix It Up.   **# of players:** Any.
Type: Icebreaker.
Supplies: Name tags for each guest, but some in green, some in red, some in yellow, etc.
Formation: Guests circulate.
Object of the game: To get to know each other.
Play action: Every so often, the leader will say, "All with a green name tag change places." The next time, another color is called, and so on.
Hints and tips: To get the conversation going quickly after the change, each name tag can have a brief comment about the person's life or hobbies.

Name of the game: Personal Bingo.   **# of players:** Any.
Type: Icebreaker.
Supplies: Oversized Bingo cards (see the pattern on page 74), one for each player. Small prizes relating to the theme.
Formation: Players are seated around the room. A table or magazines are available to support the player's card and objects.
Object of the game: To win at Bingo by removing all the items.
Play action: The players are told to take objects out of their purses or pockets, and place one object on each empty square of their Bingo card. When everyone is ready, the leader chooses someone to start. The designated person takes one article off his or her card, holds it up, and calls it out to the group, say, "lipstick." All players with a lipstick on their card can take that article off their card. The next person repeats the process, calling out an object and then removing that object from his or her card. This goes on until someone shouts "Bingo!" Decide on the configuration at the outset: vertical or horizontal, four corners, six-pack, or cover all.

Adaptation: Pocket Hunt.   **# of players:** Any.
Supplies: List of articles to ask for.
Formation: Players seated.
Object of the game: To reach a set number of items.
Play action: The leader asks for a specific object. Guests hunt through wallet, pockets, or purse for that item. The first one to reach a set number of items wins.

Variation: Can be played as couples or teams, as well as individually.

Hints and tips: Suggestions for hunt:

1. pet photo
2. pill box
3. new penny
4. nail file
5. safety pin

6. golf tee
7. postage stamp
8. stick of gum
9. unpaid bill
10. Social Security card

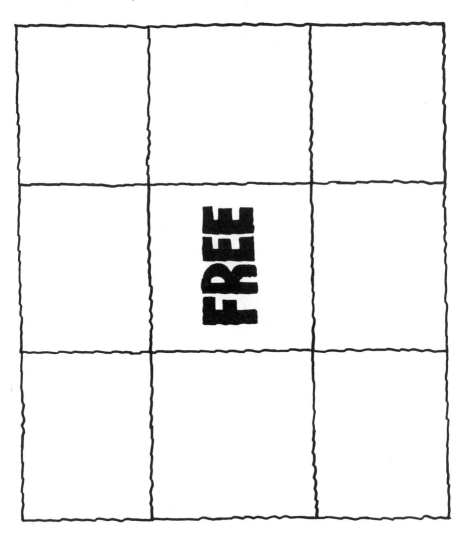

Name of the game: Sentence Mix-Ups.   **# of players:** 20 or more.

Type: Icebreaker.

Supplies: Fairly large cards, say, 4"x6" or 5"x8", with a word written on them with a black soft-tipped pen. At least twice as many cards as there are players. Candy. Prize.

Formation: Players continually mixing.

Object of the game: Players are to get together to form sentences with their words.

Play action: Players get a word card and then mingle, trying to build a complete sentence with other words. When a sentence is formed, the group reports to the leader, who takes their cards and gives each of them a piece of candy for a reward and a new word card. They go off again to make new sentences and to collect more rewards and cards. There's one rule: Sentences should not contain fewer than five words. A small prize is given to the player with the most candy at the end.

Hints and tips: The easiest way to prepare cards is to write out actual sentences and then mix them up. Always add a few extra linking words such as *a, of, the, but,* and *or.* Have plenty of word cards on hand. Also, when the players' sentences are handed in, their cards can be reshuffled and used again later on. A word can be written on both sides of the cards, making the action faster. This is a good time to use an assistant because it's difficult to judge the sentences for coherence, reshuffle cards, and hand out more cards and candy at the same time.

Adaptation: Use a letter on the cards instead of a word. Players search for two or more letters to form a word.

Name of the game: Word Builders.   **# of players:** Two teams of 12 players each.

Type: Icebreaker team contest.

Supplies: Forty-six large white cards about 5″x8″, with one letter of the alphabet written on each one in bold black letters (omit Q, X, and Z). You will need two complete sets. (26 letters − 3 = 23 x 2 = 46.)

Formation: Players are given two cards apiece (with the exception of one player who gets one card).

Object of the game: The team showing the word first wins a point.

Play action: The leader calls out a word and the players, standing in two groups, must send the correct letter arranged in the correct order to the front, presenting the word to the rest of the guests.

Hints and tips: Don't choose words with repeated letters.

Name of the game: Feelings.   **# of players:** Any.
Type: Icebreaker.
Supplies: A thick knee sock, filled with familiar objects, such as a spoon, button, safety pin, clothespin, thimble, matchbook, paper clip, votive candle, roll of tape, and key—up to about 20 items. Paper and pencil.
Formation: Casual seating.

Object of the game: To remember as many objects as possible.
Play action: Pass the sock around to the guests, giving each about a minute to feel the objects. Take the stocking away and hand out papers. Ask players to write down as many items as they can remember. The stocking is opened later for checking.
Hints and tips: If there are more than 10 players, pass two socks containing the same items around to save time.

Name of the game: Lapse of Memory.   **# of players:** Any.
Type: Icebreaker.
Supplies: Paper and pencils. Prize.
Formation: Mixing among players.
Object of the game: To record the most "lapses of memory."
Play action: Ask your guests to come to the party with something about them that indicates a lapse of memory, such as a watch worn upside down, different socks, one earring, or a shirt buttoned up incorrectly. Give out paper and pencils. Offer a prize for the greatest number of correct guesses.
Hints and tips: The game should be timed for about 10 minutes.

Name of the game: Name Bingo.   **# of players:** 24 or more.
Type: Icebreaker.
Supplies: Specially made Bingo cards (see the pattern on page 78). Beans or small stones for markers. Pencils. Prizes.
Formation: As guests arrive, they "sign in" on a slip of paper, which is put into a large jar or basket.
Object of the game: To win at Bingo.
Play action: To begin, guests circulate and collect a signature on all the blank squares of their card. Allow about 10 minutes for this. The leader stirs the slips of paper and calls out the chosen names. Bingo can be made by vertical or horizontal, four corners, diagonal, or cover-all configurations, decided beforehand.
Hints and tips: I like to suggest that the person requesting a signature should first pronounce the person's name *before* it is given.
Adaptation: To get a signature, you must introduce yourself first and tell the person one thing about yourself, such as your favorite hobby or a goal in life. Getting a signature is not an exchange. The one who takes the initiative in going to the other person gets the signature.

6
QUIET GAMES & TABLE GAMES

QUIET GAMES
• •

The following games are quiet, inactive games. They include pencil-and-paper, word, guessing, and memory games.

These are wonderful games to change the pace of a party and to stimulate your guests' thinking skills. There is usually some mental competition involved where a quick response is important. The questions or puzzles can be as hard as your group is intelligent—you will be surprised at how much everyone knows.

Name of the game: "Dis" and "De."   **# of players:** Any.
Type: Fast thinking.
Supplies: A clever mind.
Formation: Individuals seated informally or in a small circle.
Object of the game: To continue sequence.
Play action: The player must come up with two factors—first, a person's occupation, say, a pig farmer; then a circumstance must befall him that will use the prefixes "dis" or "de," as in this example: When the *pig farmer* lost his farm, he was *disgruntled*. *Pig* and *grunt* correspond for a logical answer, and *disgruntled* is an apt emotion that corresponds with him losing his farm.
Hints and tips: Other examples: When the *baker* dropped his *cake*, it was *distorted*. When the *lawyer* committed *perjury*, he was *disbarred*. When the *wizard* lost his *spell book*, he was *disenchanted*.

Name of the game: Desert Island Among Friends.   **# of players:** Five or six to a group.
Type: Pencil-and-paper.
Supplies: Paper and pencils. Timer.
Formation: Groups, each with a leader.
Object of the game: To make lists.
Play action: Each group suggests words for various foods beginning with the letter *T*, which their leader writes down. Then they do the same with a variety of drinks beginning with the letter *C*, articles of clothing also beginning with *C*, and household furnishings and utensils beginning with *St*. Allow 3 or 4 minutes for this part. One group is then selected to call out its lists and then the other groups strike out their identical answers. Another group reads its lists of "what's left" and again identical objects are eliminated. This continues until each group is left with only those items that no other group has. In the last stage, the host explains that everyone has been shipwrecked and has washed ashore on a desert island. The group leader of each island will now stand and read off what foods his or her group will live on, what they will all have to drink, what they will wear, and finally, what equipment is available for building a shelter.

Name of the game: Personal Favorites.   **# of players:** Small group.
Type: Pencil-and-paper.
Supplies: Paper and pencils.
Formation: Casual seating.
Object of the game: For fun and to get to know each other better.
Play action: The leader asks everyone to write down six things they could never have too much of. When everyone is finished, they sign their paper and pass it in to the leader. The leader reads the papers out loud while everyone tries to guess whose list is being read. Writers must confess to their own list if no one guesses.
Hints and tips: Ask for some minor elaboration on the list if possible. This is best played with a small group of friends who meet regularly or know each other fairly well.

Name of the game: Dear Santa Claus.   **# of players:** Any.
Type: Pencil-and-paper game for Christmas party.
Supplies: Paper and pencils.
Formation: Informal circle.
Object of the game: Imaginative entertainment.
Play action: All players are instructed to write a letter to Santa
   Claus for the person on their left. Allow about 8 minutes for the
   writing. Then the players will pass the letter they wrote to the
   person on their right. Start around the circle, having the play-
   ers read the letter that was passed to them.
Hints and tips: The leader should encourage originality. This
   game works best with people who know each other well and
   will be clever in their letter writing. Nothing too literal should
   be written. The spontaneity will produce hilarious results.

Name of the game: Singing Charades.   **# of players:** Four or five to a team.
Type: Pencil-and-paper.
Supplies: A list of songs prepared in advance by the games leader. Pencils and paper.
Formation: Guests divided into equal groups or teams.
Object of the game: To quickly guess the song from a drawing and win as many times as possible.
Play action: Each group sends one person to the middle of the room, where all the participants are given the name of a song. (The games leader may whisper the name or point to a written title.) The participants then run back to their team and draw a picture that best describes the song. No words can be said or written by the artist. The team tries to guess the song, and immediately sings it out when it guesses it. The first team to sing the correct song wins. Each team sends another player to get the name of another song. The game is repeated until everyone has had a turn as the group artist.
Hints and tips: It is important for each group to be situated an equal distance from the leader. The choice of songs is also very important—select songs that everyone will know.
Adaptation: You can pick songs to correspond to your party's theme. For instance, a party at Christmastime would be perfect for carols. It is usually sufficient for the group to sing only one chorus of the song, but with Christmas carols you may want to sing them all the way through.

Name of the game: False Observation.   **# of players:** Any.
Type: Pencil-and-paper.
Supplies: Paper and pencils. A tray holding an array of unrelated objects.
Formation: Casual group seating or circle.
Object of the game: Seemingly, to guess as many objects as possible.
Play action: An assistant will bring out a tray covered with a display of articles. The assistant will allow each player about 30 seconds to examine the tray. The assistant then leaves the room. The winner will be the one who guesses the most things about *the assistant*—the person carrying the tray—that he or she can remember! Examples of points: color of the person's

eyes, shirt, or blouse; type of shoes, glasses, or jewelry; mustache or beard; and hair decoration.

Hints and tips: Suggestions for tray: sewing supplies, costume jewelry, kitchen gadgets, fishing paraphernalia, and stationery or office supplies.

Adaptation: If you have played this game with the same group before, and they are wise to the instructions about identifying the assistant, or if the assistant is well known by the guests, make them actually guess the contents of the tray instead.

Name of the game: Hidden Cities **# of players:** Teams or individuals.

Type: Pencil-and-paper.

Supplies: Paper and pencils.

Formation: Comfortable seating.

Object of the game: To find the hidden or concealed cities.

Play action: Players form teams to work on writing a paragraph that will contain hidden cities. The cities may be a word, part of a word, or letters used in correct sequence to form a word—all within a story. Each team tries to write the best story and stump the others.

Hints and tips: Individuals may play this game by themselves, but since it's very difficult, a team effort is ultimately better. Allow at least 10 minutes for the writing part. The following story was written by a very bright fifth-grade class.

There once was a girl born in August at 5:00 P.M. Her name was Rosan Francisco. She was nice. She liked the lake, land, and air, but most of all she liked to watch her horse stamp around. Her best friend was another girl named Chey Ennebe. If she got mad, she threw little rocks at her brother. For shame, Rosan and Chey! Chey played softball. There was a catcher named Rouge. When Chey struck out, she threw the bat on Rouge. What a lump! Rouge was angry at Chey and did quote angry words. Chey's brother was frank, for the problem had to be solved.

The hidden cities: Augusta, San Francisco, Nice, Lakeland, Tampa, Cheyenne, Little Rock, Baton Rouge, Frankfort.

Adaptation: Points can be awarded to teams for the most cities used in their own stories, as well as the most cities found within other stories.

Name of the game: Balderdash or Not.   **# of players:** Any.
Type: Pencil-and-paper.
Supplies: List of unusual words with one correct definition and
 four false definitions. Pencils and paper.
Formation: Informal group or circle seating.
Object of the game: To have the most right definitions.
Play action: The leader reads the word aloud, making sure the
 pronunciation is correct, and then spells it out. Players copy
 the word on their paper. Then five definitions are read. The
 players choose the one they think is correct and write it under
 the word. The player with the most correct answers wins.
Hints and tips: Sometimes I take my words and their real and
 daffy definitions from the game of Balderdash, a Games Gang
 Ltd. product, which can be purchased at many book and toy
 stores. But you can get all the information you need from a
 good dictionary—if you don't mind the work. Here are some
 samples I made up myself.

(1) Scolex (sko-leks)
answers: 1. A shoot or branch used for grafting
       2. A dip on a ski run
       3. An exercise weight
       4. The head of a tapeworm
       5. Hairs on a bee's leg that gather pollen

(2) Psilocin (si-le-sin)
answers: 1. Either of two muscles in the loin
       2. Hallucinogenic compounds found in mushrooms
       3. A type of Indian seed corn
       4. A genus of vines bearing a large, edible, gobular
         fruit with a yellowish-orange rind
       5. Having a purple tinge

(3) Neologism (knee-ahle-gizm)
answers: 1. A birthmark
       2. A new word or phrase
       3. Acted in a stingy way
       4. Not involved in political-party ties, the opposite
         of patriotism
       5. New breathing in short, irregular bursts

(4) Googolplex (goo-goal-plex)
answers: 1. A building with more than a thousand windows
       2. An instrument for measuring angles

3. A river of ice in a high valley
4. Clarified semifluid butter made from water buffalo's milk
5. The figure one followed by a googol of zeroes

Answers: 1. #4, 2. #2, 3. #2, 4. #5

Name of the game: Ridiculous.   **# of players:** Small group.
Type: Pencil-and-paper.
Supplies: Prepared questions. Paper and pencils.
Formation: Sitting and writing.
Object of the game: To create amusing stories.
Play action: The leader asks players to write down responses to the following commands or questions.

1. Write a number between 1 and 150.
2. "Yes" or "no"?
3. A number, not over 20, or "none."
4. A measurement, not more than 3 yards (274 centimeters).
5. A weight, not over 350 pounds (772 kilos).
6. An occupation.
7. Another occupation.
8. A number, not over 100.
9. A sum of money.
10. Another sum of money.
11. Names of two well-known living people.
12. One vice and one virtue.

Now explain to the players that they have been filling out an employment application. Read the questions and ask for some group response:

1. What is your age?
2. Married?
3. Children, if any?
4. Height?
5. Weight?
6. Last occupation?
7. Occupation desired?
8. Years at last job?
9. Weekly salary there?
10. Salary now required?
11. References?
12. Chief characteristics, as stated by these two people?

Name of the game: Football Daffynitions.   **# of players:** Any.
Type: Pencil-and-paper.
Supplies: Pencils and paper. Prepared list of football teams and their daffynitions for leader to read.
Formation: Informal group or circle seating.
Object of the game: To guess the most correct answers.
Play action: Have players number their paper from 1 through 28. Read the daffynitions for the football teams at least twice, giving the players enough time to think each one through. The players write their football-team guesses on their paper next to the corresponding number. The player with the most correct answers wins.
Hints and tips: These daffynitions are tough. Not everyone will get them on the first go-through.

Daffynitions:

1. Rodeo animals
2. A dollar for corn
3. Ocean-going bird
4. Basic rule
5. Army insects
6. Used to be girls
7. Lubricators
8. Boy Scout title
9. King of the beasts
10. Streakers are this
11. Attacker
12. Baby toy with fish protuberances
13. Pickle company employees
14. I.O.U.'s
15. Six shooters
16. American gauchos
17. Trained to kill
18. Tanned bodies
19. Hot epidermis
20. Iron workers
21. Opposite of ewes
22. Credit-card users
23. In Louis Armstrong's song
24. Leaders of Indians

Answers:

1. Denver Broncos
2. Tampa Bay Buccaneers
3. Seattle Seahawks
4. Cardinals
5. Giants
6. Bengals
7. Houston Oilers
8. Philadelphia Eagles
9. Detroit Lions
10. Chicago Bears
11. Raiders
12. Miami Dolphins
13. Green Bay Packers
14. Buffalo Bills
15. Indianapolis Colts
16. Dallas Cowboys
17. Atlanta Falcons
18. Cleveland Browns
19. Washington Redskins
20. Pittsburgh Steelers
21. L.A. Rams
22. San Diego Chargers
23. New Orleans Saints
24. Kansas City Chiefs

25. The four Norsemen	25. Minnesota Vikings
26. A 747	26. New York Jets
27. Seven squared	27. San Francisco '49ers
28. Proud American men	28. New England Patriots

Name of the game: The Robust Letter. **# of players:** Any.
Type: Pencil-and-paper.
Supplies: A list of objects for the leader. Paper and pencils.
Formation: Informal seating with writing surface.
Object of the game: To score the most points with uncommon words.
Play action: Dictate list of objects. Players will write them down on the left side of their papers. Then select a letter from the alphabet, which will then be used as the initial letter for every one of the objects on the list. Score one point for common words and two points for words no one else has thought of.
Hints and tips: Sample list: country, occupation, vehicle, song, street name, flower, animal, tree, mineral, precious stone, town, bird, drink, author, article of clothing, furniture, girl's name, motto, and novel. If the chosen letter is *P*, possible answers could be: Peru, plumber, plow, and so on.

Name of the game: Telegram. **# of players:** Any.
Type: Pencil-and-paper.
Supplies: Paper and pencils. Timer (suggested time: 3–5 minutes).
Formation: Casual seating.
Object of the game: To create a telegram. Don't indicate this until the letters are chosen.
Play action: The leader dictates 10 letters. These are to be used as the *first letters* of 10 words on a telegram in the order that they are given. Use all the letters. For example: The letters chosen were O, P, A, T, W, M, Y, E, H, and B. This is the telegram that was created: **O**ur **P**arents **A**t **T**he **W**ayside. **M**ay **Y**ou **E**njoy **H**appy **B**irthday.
Hints and tips: Make sure you give or show the example.

Name of the game: Connected-Word Thinking. **# of players:** Any.

Type: Pencil-and-paper.

Supplies: Paper and pencils. Timer.

Formation: Sitting and writing. Can be played individually or in teams.

Object of the game: To think up the most original pairs.

Play action: A letter is chosen. Players now go through the alphabet, thinking up and writing down pairs of connected words, with the second word in the pair beginning with the chosen letter. Here are some examples with the letter **C**:

- Alternating **C**urrent
- Before **C**hrist
- Complex **C**arbohydrates
- District of **C**olumbia

When "time" is called, players read out their lists and strike out any pairs that have been read by others. The winner is the one (or team) with the most original pairs.

Hints and Tips: You may need another judge for a second opinion as to what pairs are legitimate.

Name of the game: Wink (or Murder). **# of players:** Small group.

Type: Group intrigue.

Supplies: Deck of cards.

Formation: Players sitting in a circle, with everyone having a clear view of one another.

Objects of the game: Two: The murderer tries to kill off the entire group, and a player spots the murderer and stops him.

Play action: The card deck is fixed so that there is one card for each player, and one of the cards is a joker. The person who draws the joker card is the murderer. All take and return their cards secretly. The murderer then begins his killing. This is accomplished by the wink of an eye, which is quick, silent, and undetected by everyone except "the victim." The player who receives the wink should hesitate a moment or two (so as not to give anything away) and then utter a sigh or groan and declare himself dead. The surviving players venture a guess as to who the murder is—before he kills again! But a false accusation is more than slander; it is instant death itself!

Name of the game: Newspaper Reporter.   **# of players:** Any.
Type: Pencil-and-paper.
Supplies: Newspaper, colored pens, and paper. Timer. Prize.
Formation: Enough room for each player to spread out newspaper and write.
Object of the game: To make the best sentence possible. Don't disclose until the first task is complete.
Play action: Each player is given a sheet of newspaper, a piece of paper, and a colored pen. Competitors are instructed to start at the top of the first column of print and find a word beginning with *A*. A ring is drawn around the *A* word, and the word is noted on their paper. Then the search is continued on through the alphabet, but omitting *X* and *Z*. In this game, proper names and awkward words should not be avoided. Allow 5 minutes for this part of the game. Those players who do not complete their list must do without the remaining letters, so stress the time a bit. For the second part of the game, players now have to make up the most intelligible sentence they can from the words they have written down in their list, using them *in any order*. Allow 3 minutes for this. Then the competitors read their sentence out loud. The winner of the game is the one who has used up the greatest number of words in his or her list in the most reasonable sentence.

Name of the game: Mixed-Up Mottos.   **# of players:** Any.
Type: Pencil-and-paper.
Supplies: Slips of paper prepared in advance with a mixed-up motto or proverb on them—one for each player. Paper and pencils. Timer.
Formation: Players sit in a circle.
Object of the game: To decipher a motto.
Play action: Each player is given a piece of paper with a "potted proverb" written on it—that is, with the consonants strung together and all the vowels omitted. After 30 seconds, the leader calls "change," whether the proverb or motto is deciphered or not, and the players pass their papers to the left. Those who decipher a motto score a point. The game continues until all the players have seen all the slips.
Hints and tips: Example: **LKBFYLP,** for **"LOOK BEFORE YOU LEAP."**

Name of the game: Numbers Are.   **# of players:** Any.
Type: Pencil-and-paper.
Supplies: Prepared lists. Pencils. Timer. Prize (optional).
Formation: Seating in teams or worked as individuals.
Object of the game: The most correct answers at "Time."
Play action: Players are to guess the words associated with the numbers. Giving them one example will make this clear.

1. 26 = L of the A
2. 1001 = A N
3. 12 = S of the Z
4. 54 = C in a D (with the J)
5. 9 = P in the S S
6. 88 = P K
7. 13 = S on the A F
8. 32 = DF at which W F
9. 18 = H on a G C
10. 90 = D in a R A
11. 3 = B M (S H T R)

12. 4 = Q in a G
13. 24 = H in a D
14. 1 = W on a U
15. 5 = D in a Z C
16. 57 = H V
17. 11 = P on a F T
18. 29 = D in F in a L Y
19. 64 = S on a C
20. 40 = D and N of the G F
21. 7 = W of the A W

Answers:

1. Letters of the Alphabet
2. Arabian Nights
3. Signs of the Zodiac
4. Cards in a Deck with the Jokers
5. Planets in the Solar System
6. Piano Keys
7. Stripes on the American Flag
8. Degrees Fahrenheit at which Water Freezes
9. Holes on a Golf Course
10. Degrees in a Right Angle
11. Blind Mice (See How They Run)
12. Quarts in a Gallon
13. Hours in a Day
14. Wheel on a Unicycle
15. Digits in a Zip Code
16. Heinz Varieties
17. Players on a Football Team
18. Days in February in a Leap Year
19. Squares on a Checkerboard
20. Days and Nights of the Great Flood
21. Wonders of the Ancient World

Name of the game: Tell a Truth.   **# of players:** Any.
Type: Story telling.
Supplies: Toilet-paper roll.
Formation: Casual group or circle seating.
Object of the game: To get better acquainted and exercise creativity.
Play action: A roll of toilet paper is passed around and guests are told to take as much or as little as they like. After they all have their amount, they must tell one fact about themselves for each sheet of paper they hold.
Adaptation: A ball of yarn is used and each player is told to cut off an ample amount. After the yarn is all given out, its use is disclosed. Each person is to talk about his- or herself. As they speak they wind the yarn around their index finger. If they have taken a large piece, they probably have to talk longer than they like. If they try to talk slowly and wind fast, it will not be easy. If they pause to think, the winding must stop also. The minute the yarn runs out, they must stop talking, even if in midsentence.

TABLE GAMES
• •

These are party games where people are seated around a table or need to make use of a table.

Name of the game: Resolutions (New Year's).   **# of players:** Any.
Type: Table game.
Supplies: Paper and pencil.
Formation: Seated at a table or in a circle.
Object of the game: Fun reading.
Play action: Each guest writes down a New Year's resolution. Allow a couple of minutes for this. Then each folds the paper to hide the resolution, and passes it to someone two places to his or her left. The next part to be written is the reason for the resolution. Pass the papers again and this player reads the outcome.
Hints and tips: Phrase the reading like this: "I am going to do _____ (the resolution) because _____ (the reason)."

Name of the game: Ping-Pong Blow.   **# of players:** Teams of 8 to 10.

Type: Table game.

Supplies: Ping-Pong balls and table (long banquet table or smooth picnic table).

Formation: Two teams on opposite sides of the table.

Object of the game: To score 21 points.

Play action: Two teams sit or kneel on opposite sides of the table. Players keep their hands behind their backs. A Ping-Pong ball is dropped in the middle of the table by the leader or assistant, and players are instructed to blow the ball across the table and off the edge of the other side, scoring a point for their own team. All balls going off the end of the table are dropped in the middle again.

Hints and tips: An assistant is valuable here.

Adaptation: Use straws for blowing.

Name of the game: Map It Out.   **# of players:** Four or five on a team.
Type: Table game.
Supplies: One map of the same state for each team. One pencil for each captain.
Formation: Teams are gathered around a map on a table. They select a team captain.
Object of the game: To spot location of cities first.
Play action: The leader calls out the name of a city. The group hunts for it on the map. When found, the captain must draw a circle around it and raise his or her pencil high in the air. The first hand to go up wins one point for his or her team. Go for a total number of points, say, 15.
Hints and tips: The leader needs to be able to see each group to determine the winner easily. Also, make sure that your maps have their index guides cut off or folded under. (Every year the tourist commission sends maps to me in the mail for *free*.)
Adaptation: For your more intelligent friends or for a travel club, why not try maps of the world for more of a challenge.

Name of the game: Steal-a-Gift.   **# of players:** Small groups of five or six.
Type: Table game.
Supplies: One pair of dice for each group or table. One gift per person.
Formation: Small group of people around a card table. A stack of small gifts (enough for each player) are in the middle of the table. Timer.
Object of the game: To get and keep as many gifts as possible before time is called.
Play action: Players take turns rolling the dice—one roll at a time and only once. If they throw a 7 or 11, they get to take one gift from the gift pile. When these gifts are gone, they can go to another table and steal a gift from its pile. If they roll a double 1 (snake eyes) or a double six (boxcars), they must *return* a gift to the pile if they have one. Try for a 10-minute game.
Hints and tips: Remember to keep a close watch on the time. Consider the competitiveness and maturity of the players carefully. Fast action.

Name of the game: Penny Ante.   **# of players:** Any.
Type: Table or banquet game.
Supplies: Glasses, napkins, musical cues.
Formation: Guests seated at one or more banquet tables.
Object of the game: To not get caught.
Play action: Guests are asked to place all their pennies on the table in front of them. Music begins. As the music plays, a glass (lined with a napkin) is passed around from one player to the next. When the music stops, whoever is holding the glass drops in a penny. The ante is raised to a nickel after three or four rounds. Players are led to believe that the next ante will be a quarter. The glass travels more rapidly now, and when the music stops, the victim is ready to pay, but is surprised to find out that he or she may pocket all the money.
Hints and tips: Recorded music will do as well as a pianist. Vary the directions in regards to the task. For example, the one caught may be instructed to take out one penny or to put two in or to give one to someone at the table.

7
RELAYS, MUSICAL ACTIVITIES & STUNTS

ACTIVE GAMES AND RELAYS

Active games are best for casual get-togethers, where people are dressed informally. They are often played at picnics, barbecues, or other functions where there is plenty of room. Active games may be indoor or outdoor, and some cross over into both categories.

Relays are usually simple tasks everyone is capable of doing, but it is the team camaraderie coupled with the fast time element that make them so challenging and fun.

Name of the game: Pass the Orange.   **# of players:** Two teams.
Type: Team relay.
Supplies: Oranges, one for each team. Chairs.
Formation: Competitors are seated in two rows facing one another.
Object of the game: To be the first team to finish.
Play action: An orange is started at one end and it carefully travels the length of the row by being passed along on the tops of player's feet. A dropped orange must be introduced two people back.
Hints and tips: Legs must be kept quite stiff and tilted slightly to drop the orange gently onto the next pair of feet. This game should not be rushed.

Name of the game: Chin-to-Chin.   **# of players:** Two teams.
Type: Team relay.
Supplies: Either an orange or a tennis ball.
Formation: Two lines of alternating men and women.
Object of the game: To finish first.
Play action: On a signal, an orange is given to the first player in
   both lines. They tuck it under their chin and pass it on through
   the line, chin to chin. Suggest that players clasp their hands
   behind their back, because "no hands" are allowed. Should the
   orange fall, it must be reintroduced *one person back* from where
   it fell.

Name of the game: Spoons.   **# of players:** Any.
Type: Active indoor.
Supplies: Regular playing cards, spoons.
Formation: Players sit on the floor in a circle. Spoons (one less than the number of players) are in a pile in the middle, an equal distance from all the players. The deck of cards is prepared using four cards of a kind for every player. For example, if there were five players, the deck could be made up of four aces, four kings, four queens, four jacks, and four tens.
Object of the game: To grab a spoon.
Play action: Cards are mixed and after the deal, if no one player has four of a kind, they all pass one card to their left at the same time. They continue passing cards until a player gets four of a kind (like four kings); then that player stops passing and grabs a spoon. As other players notice this, they grab for a spoon also. The odd man out does not get a spoon.
Hints and tips: This game gets wild and furious. Care should be taken with long fingernails and pointy rings.
Adaptation: A longer version (good for a fewer number of players) is, the one who does not get a spoon in three rounds is out.

Name of the game: People String Along.   **# of players:** Teams of five or six players.
Type: Relay.
Supplies: One ball of string, with a spoon tied to the end—for each team.
Formation: Single-file line-up for each team.
Object of the game: To complete the team race first.
Play action: On "Go," the first player passes the spoon down the front of his shirt and through his pants and lets it come out his pants' leg. The spoon is then passed on to the next player, all the while with more string being released. As soon as the spoon has reached the end and all the players are connected, the last player pulls the spoon back and the process is reversed, with the first player winding in a little string each time the spoon travels up the person and thus up the line. The winners are the first team to have the spoon travel down and back up the line, ending up with the string wound back in a ball, and the team signalling its completion by sitting down.
Hints and tips: Obviously players should be wearing sports clothes. Broken string disqualifies. Great holiday stress-defuser.

Name of the game: Variety Relay.   **# of players:** Any.
Type: Couples relay.
Supplies: Crackers, balloons, potatoes, chairs (one for each couple). Designated familiar song.
Formation: A line of women opposite a line of men, about 30 feet apart; chairs on the men's side.
Object of the game: To complete a series of tasks, men first, next women, and then the two together.
Play action: On "Go": (1) Each man eats his cracker, runs to his female partner, kneels before her, and whistles the designated tune. (2) When the woman guesses the correct tune, she, (3) blows up her balloon, knots it, runs to a chair, and sits on the balloon to pop it. When popped, she runs back, joining her partner. (4) They then place a potato between their foreheads and move across the floor to the chair. If the potato falls, they must start from their beginning point again. To signal their finish, the woman sits down and the man stands beside her chair.
Hints and tips: A different song could be whispered to each man when given his cracker. Explain and partially demonstrate the relay sequence at the outset.

Name of the game: Roll Along.   **# of players:** Any.
Type: Team relay.
Supplies: Chairs, string, Ping-Pong balls.
Formation: One player from each team is seated. His or her teammates are standing about 4 feet away.
Object of the game: To roll the Ping-Pong ball along the string without dropping it.
Play action: One player holds the ends of a long double string and the first seated player takes the other ends and holds the strings very taut and somewhat separated. The Ping-Pong ball is placed on the string and made to slide along the string to the end and back again by changing the slope of the strings.
Hints and tips: Speed is not always a good idea because the ball can roll off the player's hands at the turnaround point.

Name of the game: Waiter Please.   **# of players:** Any.
Type: Team relay.
Supplies: Ping-Pong balls and plates.

Formation: Two teams standing with a good space between each player.

Object of the game: To hurry through serving breakfast.

Play action: The first player carries a plate with a Ping-Pong ball on it (this is the "breakfast egg"). He must run in and out of his teammates, declaring to each, "Your breakfast egg is here, Sir (or Madam)." When this player's rounds are finished, it's passed on to the next player, waiter #2, and so on.

Name of the game: Crazy Bowling.   **# of players:** Any.

Type: Relay (team or individuals).

Supplies: Tennis balls. A chalk-drawn target is drawn at one end of the floor in a large room (or you can use masking tape).

Formation: Players stand behind a line a distance away from the target.

Object of the game: To score the most points.

Play action: This is a type of bowling with tennis balls.

Hints and tips: Possible target:

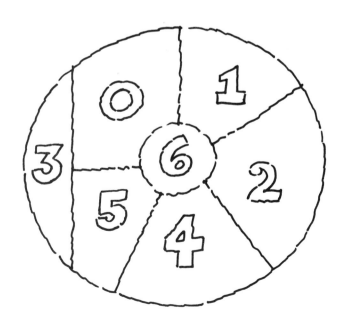

Name of the game: Fish-Pool Relay.   **# of players:** Less than 18 in groups of 3.
Type: Team relay.
Supplies: A chalk-drawn "pool" (or you can use masking tape) in a large room. Colored-construction-paper fish and fans (which can also be made of folded newspapers) for each team.
Formation: Each player standing between 20 and 40 feet from the pool, and in three groups as if they were points on a triangle with the pool in the middle.
Object of the game: To get the fish back into their pool.
Play action: Each team sends out a player to fan their fish back into the pool. Once in, the first player runs back and hands his or her fan to the second player. (Any fish that are fanned out must be fanned back in for a win!)
Hints and tips: Each team should have different-colored fish to make scoring easier. You can use the target drawn from the previous game, Crazy Bowling, to make this game more difficult.

Name of the game: Playing-Card Race.   **# of players:** Any.
Type: Team relay.
Supplies: A pack of playing cards for each team.
Formation: Teams facing one another.
Object of the game: To work through the deck first, in order.
Play action: The leader names a suit. The first player in the team must go through the pack until he finds the ace in that suit. The pack is passed to the second player, who goes through it and selects the 2 card of that suit. This is done all the way through the deck—ace, 2, 3 . . . up to jack, queen, and king. The first team finished wins.

Name of the game: Winner.   **# of players:** Any.
Type: Team relay.
Supplies: Prepare about a hundred small alphabet cards, cut up from index cards, each containing one letter of the alphabet.
Formation: The men of the team run forward.
Object of the game: To find the word "winner."
Play action: Cards are scattered face down on a table. Men are to run backwards to the table and look for the letters in the word

"winner" one at a time. They must pick up a letter, look at it, and replace it face down if it is not the letter they want.

Hints and tips: The correct letters should be held up and shown to the leader or assistant to keep track of each team's progress.

MUSICAL ACTIVITIES

There are many versions of the elementary-school game of Musical Chairs. These games obviously require music for cues and an object to be manipulated until there is an "odd man out." They are still as much fun as you remember as a child and the different possibilities are endless.

Name of the game: Music Me a Balloon.   **# of players:** Six or more.

Type: Active music.

Supplies: Record or cassette or live piano music. Balloons, enough for all but one player.

Formation: The players are standing in a circle. The leader is at the record player (or cassette player or piano).

Object of the game: To be holding a balloon when the music stops.

Play action: As the music plays, all players will pass their balloons in the same direction. When the music suddenly stops, the player without a balloon is out.

Hints and tips: A balloon is removed with each player out, and all players holding a popped balloon are also out.

Adaptation: Music Me a Hat: Players will move hats instead of balloons. They may reach over and remove the hat from the person sitting or standing next to them, instead of waiting for the pass.

Adaptation: Music Me a Gift: Players are sitting in a circle. A gift wrapped many times over is circulated around the circle to music. When the music stops, the player holding the gift unwraps it until the music starts again, and then he or she must pass it on. The person who unwraps the gift completely wins that gift. Plan on using more than one gift at a time for greater excitement and motivation.

STUNTS AND FORFEITS

Stunts are great for a change of pace. The best players will often be people whom you know to be good sports. Stunts are the most fun when other guests are on the sidelines watching. They will have as much fun as the participants themselves.

In terms of forfeit games, there are positive ways of incorporating "victims" or losers into a party. For instance, ask them to pay a compliment to each guest there, or to make a 2-minute speech "in praise of yourself." Never try to humiliate the victim of a forfeit or make him or her feel like the butt of a joke.

Name of the game: Socks and Gloves.   **# of players:** About five or six.

Type: Stunt.

Supplies: Several pairs of stockings and socks. Several pairs of thick gloves, like oven mitts, fur-lined gloves, garden or work gloves, and mittens. Blindfolds for each player. Timer.

Formation: Small circle of players, with others watching. Socks in a pile in the middle.

Object of the game: To wear as many socks as possible.

Play action: Players are instructed to put a glove on each hand; they should not be a matched pair. The leader and assistant then blindfold the players. On a signal, the players locate the pile of socks in the middle of the circle and put on as many as they can before time is called.

Hints and tips: You may not need a timer, because feet will only accommodate so many pairs of socks.

Name of the game: Tough Guy.   **# of players:** Six or less.

Type: Stunt.

Supplies: A full double sheet of newspaper for each player. Wet paper towels for cleaning off newsprint.

Formation: Players standing.

Object of the game: To finish first.

Play action: Players hold their arm out to the side, at shoulder height. They hold paper *at one corner only*. On a signal, they attempt to wad up the entire sheet into their fist, without lowering their arm. When finished, they raise their arm up over their head.

Name of the game: Walk the Line.   **# of players:** Any.
Type: Forfeit and stunt.
Supplies: Masking tape, binoculars.
Formation: One player performs, with others watching.
Object of the game: To walk unaffected.
Play action: Lay a masking-tape line on the floor. Ask someone to walk it, one foot in front of the other. Now, ask that player to do it again—looking through *the wrong end* of a pair of binoculars.

Name of the game: To Your Health.   **# of players:** Any.
Type: Drinking game and stunt.
Supplies: Table filled with *small* glasses of drinks. Drum. Flower.
Formation: Players seated around a table.
Object of the game: To get high.
Play action: A drummer with his back to the group slowly bangs a drum. To the drumbeat, a flower is passed from player to player. When the banging stops, the player holding the flower goes to the table, takes a drink, and finishes its contents. Play till glasses are emptied.
Hints and tips: Especially good for convention parties where there is no driving to be done later.

Name of the game: Driver's Test.   **# of players:** Any.
Type: Stunt.
Supplies: Prepared sheets with a road pattern (see the sample on the opposite page). Mirror. Pencil.
Formation: The driver sits at a table.
Object of the game: To drive the course as well as possible.
Play action: The paper with the road pattern is laid on the table in front of the player. The leader holds another sheet of paper over the road pattern so that the driver cannot look down at it directly. By looking at a mirror placed at the top of the road-pattern sheet, the driver will try to navigate the course with a pencil (or chalk).
Hints and tips: The leader, acting as a policeman, may give tickets for the driver going off the road, touching a line, and so on.

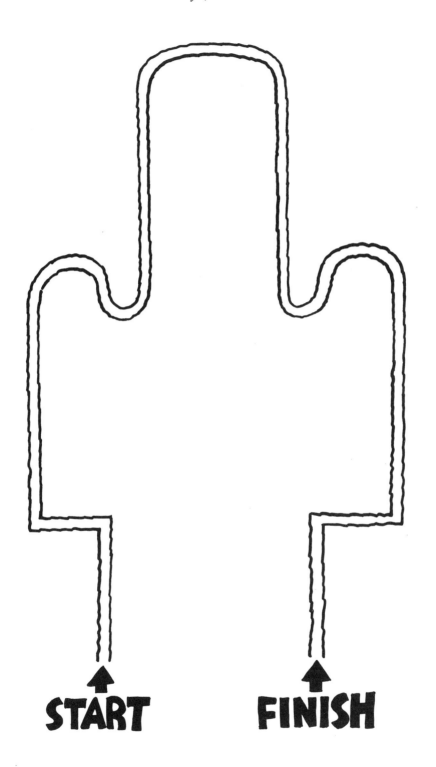

Name of the game: Words—More!   **# of players:** Any.
Type: Forfeit or contest.
Supplies: Prepared list (or dictated list). Pencils. Timer.
Formation: Sitting and writing.
Object of the game: To set a record or beat the other players.
Play action: Write down as many as you can in 3 minutes.
Hints and tips: *List suggestions:*

- words of one syllable containing double *s*
- words ending in *our*
- words of more than four syllables
- words beginning or ending with *o*
- words containing three *e*'s
- words ending in *k*
- adjectives beginning with *b*

Sample answers:
- Words of one syllable containing double *s*:
  1. pass
  2. class
  3. mass
  4. lass
  5. crass

- Words ending in *our*:
  1. sour
  2. dour
  3. hour
  4. flour
  5. tour

- Words of more than four syllables:
  1. encyclopedia
  2. subsidiary
  3. subterranean
  4. supercilious
  5. unintelligible

- Words beginning or ending with *o*:
  1. order
  2. omit
  3. ocean
  4. tomato
  5. radio

- Words containing three *e*'s:
  1. telephone
  2. evidence
  3. excessive
  4. depreciate
  5. excitement

- Words ending in *k*:
  1. kick
  2. trick
  3. sick
  4. black
  5. track

- Adjectives beginning with *b*:
  1. beautiful
  2. boastful
  3. bleak
  4. barren
  5. big

Name of the game: Van Gogh. **# of players:** Any.
Type: Forfeit and stunt.
Supplies: Paper and pencils.
Formation: Casual seating with writing surface.
Object of the game: To draw a self-portrait.
Play action: Players are given paper and pencil and asked to draw a self-portrait. Now, turn off the lights.

Name of the game: Feathers. **# of players:** Any.
Type: Forfeit.
Supplies: Feather (light enough to be blown about).
Formation: Casual seating in a small circle.
Object of the game: To avoid being "the victim."
Play action: Simple: A feather is thrown into the air and only furious blowing will keep it from landing on *you*. If it settles on you, you're the victim.

8
SHOWER & PAIRING GAMES, HUNTS & EVENTS

GAMES FOR SHOWERS

Showers are often given with the pretext of showering the honored person with gifts. These presents are meant to equip the woman getting married or having a child for the first time with much-needed items for what is about to happen in her life. Consequently, showers are not usually given for the birth of a second child. But a nice way to get around this convention would be to have a party *honoring* the woman—celebrating this important milestone in her life. At this party, I would not expect guests to bring gifts; instead, they will play games that are appropriate for the occasion and make them all feel part of the celebration.

Name of the game: Nursery-Room Drawings.   **# of players:** Small groups.
Type: Baby shower.
Supplies: 4″ x 6″ blank index cards, numbered in the bottom corner. Paper and pencils. Prizes.
Formation: Area for relaxed drawing, then for mixing.
Object of the game: To create the most successful and/or the best drawing.
Play action: Players are given blank numbered cards and asked to make a drawing that represents a well-known nursery rhyme. Allow 5 minutes for this. Then place finished drawings around the room. Players are given paper to record their selections for the most successful and/or the best drawings.

Name of the game: Diaper Cross.   **# of players:** Any.
Type: Baby shower.
Supplies: One diaper pin for each guest. Prize.
Formation: Casual mingling.
Object of the game: To collect diaper pins.
Play action: As the guests arrive, a diaper pin is pinned on their collar. As the party progresses, if one guest catches another guest crossing her legs, she may steal that guest's pin and pin it on herself. This is usually played throughout the entire party and, just before the end, the guest wearing the most pins gets a prize.
Hints and tips: It is extremely difficult to *not* cross your legs!
Adaptation: You can substitute clothespins for diaper pins for a wedding shower.

Name of the game: Sneaky Sentences.   **# of players:** Small group.
Type: Shower game and conversation fun.
Supplies: Two verbal or gregarious volunteers. Prize(s).

Formation: Two players leave the room just momentarily.
Object of the game: To create clever conversation.
Play action: While the two enlisted players are out of the room, decide upon two sentences, one for each of them. Then privately tell each one what his or her sentence is, and explain that the two of them must carry on a conversation and include their individual secret sentence as comfortably and naturally as possible.
Hints and tips: The sentences must be colorful but not too long. All will be listening for their use. If the players work their sentences into the conversation ingeniously, they deserve a prize!

Name of the game: Slogans for the Famous.   **# of players:** Any.
Type: Shower and paper-and-pencil game.
Supplies: Paper and pencils.
Formation: Casual sitting and writing.
Object of the game: To make up an appropriate and interesting slogan.
Play action: A famous living person is selected. Everyone writes the name down and then players are asked to write a slogan or a motto relating to that person. They should not use more than eight words. However, the initials of the words must be selected from the letters of the person's name. Allow 5 minutes and read the best.
Hints and tips: Example: **ANDY ROONEY**—**A**nother **N**ewsworthy **D**ocumentary **Y**et **R**uined **O**ver **O**bviously **N**othing.

Name of the game: Storyteller.   **# of players:** Any.
Type: Shower, forfeit, and contest.
Supplies: A paper bag containing five unrelated articles. Timer.
Formation: If played as a team contest, elect an unbiased judge and have two bags and a representative from each team.
Object of the game: To create a story using the contents of the bag.
Play action: Speaking talent and quick thinking are required of the players, whose stories should be enthusiastically received by the group. Allow for about 2 minutes or more for preparation.
Adaptation: Allow no time for advance preparation, making it a total ad-lib story situation.

Name of the game: Dear Advice Columnist.   **# of players:** Any.
Type: Bridal shower and pencil-and-paper game.
Supplies: Two pads of paper: white and colored. Pencils. Large hat.
Formation: Casual seating, writing.
Object of the game: To come up with frivolous and witty responses.
Play action: Pass out the white paper. On this, the players write out a question directed to an "advice columnist." The questions should be like those found in women's magazines asking for advice about love, sex, health, or money. The questions are put into a hat or large bowl, mixed, and then everyone draws one out. Next, hand out the colored paper, on which players will answer the question they drew out of the hat. Then all papers are tossed back into the hat and mixed well. The players take turns acting as "advice columnist," drawing out two papers, one white and one colored, and reading the question and the advice given.
Hints and tips: This game often produces hilarious results.

Name of the game: One-Minute Words.   **# of players:** Small group of about 12.
Type: Shower game.
Supplies: Paper and pencils for scorekeeping.
Formation: Casual seating.
Object of the game: To say as many words as possible.
Play action: In the space of one minute, the players must say as many words as they can think of that begin with a particular letter, say, *D*. As part of the challenge, derivatives must not be used because they are difficult to count and keep track of. For example, players cannot say "Drive, drove, driven, driver. . . ." Proper names are okay.

Name of the game: Cartoonists.   **# of players:** Small group.
Type: Shower.
Supplies: Paper and pencil.
Formation: Circle seating for drawing.
Object of the game: Guessing fun.
Play action: The leader asks each player to make a drawing of the head and face of the person on her left. As these drawings are turned in, she will number them and make a note as to who

they represent. The drawings are then passed around the circle and the players guess who the caricatures represent, writing down their guesses on a piece of paper. Finally, the leader transfers the names under the drawings, holds them up for all to see, and then delivers them to the subjects.

Name of the game: Decorate a Banana, Potato.   **# of players:** Any.

Type: Shower activity.

Supplies: Colored paper, pins, cotton balls, sequins, beads, soft-tipped pens, sewing embellishments like lace and cording, scissors, knives, and either bananas or potatoes. Prize(s).

Formation: Seated around large worktable, with waste can nearby.

Object of the game: To create dolls, objects, furniture, toys, etc.

Play action: Each guest gets a potato or a banana and about 20 minutes time. Give a prize for the most creative or comical results. Participants can even vote for the winners themselves.

Hints and tips: This activity often reveals a person's ingenuity, hidden artistic skills, and originality. Have banana splits or baked potatoes with all the toppings to complete the theme!

Adaptation: You can use pipe cleaners instead of food base items.

HUNTS
• •

Hunts are a unique type of party entertainment—especially if you and your friends like the idea of a good search, you have a large room or house, and you don't mind guests exploring it on their own.

Name of the game: Sentence-Clue Hunt.   **# of players:** Small group of about 12.
Type: Hunt.
Supplies: Write a long sentence indicating where a treasure is hidden. Cut it apart. Hide the sentence parts all over the room (or house).
Formation: Players seek out clues.
Object of the game: To find all the clues and piece them together.
Play action: Players collect clues and assemble them for instructions on where the treasure can be found.
Hints and tips: This type of hunt should lead to a "treasure" to be shared by all, say, a cake, bags of candy, or party favors of some sort.
Adaptation: Letter Hunt.
Supplies: Letters tied or stuck to room objects, like a lamp shade, the top of a clock, under a vase, etc. List. Paper and pencils.
Formation: Players hunt.
Object of the game: To find clues, piece them together, and find a treasure.
Play action: Participants play from a list of room objects. These room objects have letter clues on them. Players locate the objects with their attached letters and eventually piece them together to form a word or words leading to the treasure.

Name of the game: Item-by-Item Hunt.   **# of players:** Large group of about 50.
Type: Hunt and icebreaker.
Supplies: Previous party arrangements. Prize: a large candy bar.
Formation: Guests mingle.
Object of the game: To find all the objects in their *proper order* (players are on their honor).
Play action: Arrangements are made with six people privately before the party begins. They are each to represent a different object, say, (1) a sponge, (2) a capuchin monkey, (3) a pumpkin

pie, (4) a Supreme Court judge, (5) a Belgian waffle, and (6) a bar of chocolate. You will explain the game and what their respective roles are. Everyone else has to find out who these six people are, working their way from one to the other, until #6 has been reached. Person #6 has the prize: the bar of chocolate candy. The players are told that the first thing they have to find is a sponge, and that the sponge will tell them what to look for next. So everyone says to everyone else, "Are you a sponge?" When the sponge is found by a player, the sponge whispers to the player, "Right. Now look for a capuchin monkey." The capuchin monkey when found will whisper, "Yes. Now look for a pumpkin pie," and so on.

EVENTS

Often an entire party can be set up around one single "event." A popular event for a party is the game Bunko, which involves a lot of mixing and several rounds of play, so an entire party can revolve around this one game. Although Bunko involves some preparation, once it is set up and the players begin, little direction is needed.

The second event included here is Shogum, a takeoff on the old scavenger-hunt idea, but no collecting of items is involved. For a successful Shogum event, a good deal of creative thinking and advance preparation is required.

Name of the game: Bunko.   **# of players:** Twelve people or even numbers of fours.

Type: Event.

Supplies: Card tables and chairs—one table for every four players. Three dice per table. A bell. A stuffed-animal bear. Hole punchers. Score pads for tables and individual score sheets (see the pattern on page 116) for each player. At least two prizes.

Formation: Four players per table. Tables in a line and numbered 1, 2, 3, 4 (or 5). A bell at the head table, table #1. Players will rotate after each round. Winners of each round will move to the next highest table. So winners from table #4 will move to table #3, those from table #3 to table #2, and so on. (Winners from table #1 remain where they are.) The losers from table #1 (*the only losers to move*) go to the last table, table #4. The remaining players at each table, those that *lose the round*, stay at their

Name:		
Round #		
1		
2		
3		
4		
5		
6		
7		
8		
9		
10		
11		
12		
13		
14		
15		
16		
17		
18		
19		
20		

original table, *but change partners.* (Your partner is the person sitting across from you for one round of play only.)

Object of the game: You try, with your partner's help, to roll 21 points, or the most points at your table, to win the round. When the partners at the head table, table #1, roll 21 points, they will ring the bell located there and all rolling stops for everyone for that round.

Play action: Someone is designated to keep score for the table. The head table signals "Go" by ringing the bell and everyone begins to play. One player picks up the three dice and starts rolling for "ones." Every time a "one" shows up on the dice, the scorekeeper gives that team one point (a stroke tally) on the scorecard. If no "ones" are rolled, the dice must be passed to the player on the left. The neighbor on the left then begins rolling "ones" for himself and his partner. If no "ones" show up, the dice are passed again. Now, say the next player rolls three "ones." That scores five points plus any "ones" rolled from the first player, and on up to 21 points. As long as you keep rolling "ones," you can keep rolling the dice. Remember, as an added bonus, if three of the same number are rolled, you get five points and you may hold the Bunko bear. To do that, leave your seat (run!) and go to steal the bear from whomever has it, come back to your table, and then continue rolling. When the bell rings (which happens when the head table scores 21 total points), the round is over. Winners punch one hole in their individual score sheets and change tables, and losers just change seats. On the next round, players shoot for "twos" and so on, up to "sixes," and then start over again rolling for "ones."

Hints and tips: The action is fast—the comments are priceless.

Adaptation: There are many versions of this game; this one is just the easiest to explain.

Name of the game: Shogum.   **# of players:** Groups of 4 with 16 or more players.

Type: Event.

Supplies: Nine or ten businesses, areas, or landmarks in your town must be chosen and visited, and clues must be written. (Examples from my own city are cited below.) Paper, pencils, and a first clue are provided for each group. Timer. Prizes (optional).

Formation: Four team players to a car. Cars leave at 10-minute intervals. Leader will log their departure time and odometer mileage on their car.

Object of the game: To visit all locations, by deciphering clues, in as short a time and with as little mileage as possible.

Play action: The first clue given to each carload will indicate a familiar city destination. Once they reach that destination, they will see a second clue posted there, which they need to solve in order to be led to the next destination point, and so on. The first team with both the lowest mileage and total search time is the winner.

Hints and tips: There is a lot of advance preparation involved in making up rhymes, staking out locations, and coordinating cars and results, but the game is well worth the effort. Shogum examples from the game for my own city:

- Clue: "Let us put you into the driver's seat." Destination: car-rental company at the local airport.
- Clue: "Roll it up & roll it up and throw it in a pan." Destination: Patty Cake bakery.
- Clue: "If bartering is your game, William is his name." Destination: Trader Bill's pawnshop.
- Clue: "115 years of natural refreshment." Destination: Mountain Valley water building.
- Clue: "Lonesome soldier." Destination: statue landmark.
- Clue: "Charlie Brown says, 'It pays.'" Destination: Met Life office.
- Clue: "Jeeper's creepers. Where'd you get those peepers?" Destination: Mr. Peeper's Optical.
- Clue: "Today's Heartbeat of America." Destination: Allen Tillery Chevrolet.

FORMING PARTNERS, GROUPS, AND TEAMS

• •

The following devices for forming partners, groups, or teams can be used as games themselves.

Name of the game: Three of a Kind.   **# of players:** Any.
Type: Grouping and thinking.
Supplies: Slips of paper—one clue for each player
Formation: Grouping individuals into threes.
Object of the game: To find the people with the matching answer.
Play action: A separate clue is handed to each player. They must find the other guests whose answer or solution matches their own. The solution is one simple word.
Hints and tips: Examples:

1. Pillar and _____
   Mail
   Hang a notice
2. Leading actor
   Five or six points
   Asterisk
3. Part of a dress
   Do exercises
   Railroad cars
4. It hides the zipper
   A nuisance at picnics
   Ball batted high
5. Pointed wings, forked tail
   Suppress pride
   Action of throat
6. Twig
   Piece of gum
   Cling; adhere
7. Cushion
   Enter fraudulently
   Water-lily leaf

8. Fuel for fire
   A seaman's journal
   Make a note of
9. Musical tube
   Means of smoking
   Oil carrier
10. Lean sideways
    Series of items
    Retail price
11. Average
    Bad-tempered
    Intend
12. Guide rope
    Be ahead
    Conduct a band
13. Resonant sound
    Circular band
    Group
14. Strike lightly
    Dance
    Spigot

Answers: 1. Post, 2. Star, 3. Train, 4. Fly, 5. Swallow,
   6. Stick, 7. Pad, 8. Log, 9. Pipe, 10. List, 11. Mean,
   12. Lead, 13. Ring, 14. Tap.

Name of the game: Proverb Mate.   **# of players:** Any.
Type: Pairing and Icebreaker.
Supplies: Cut-in-half 3″ x 5″ index cards (one full card for each pair). Hat or basket.
Formation: Mingling.
Object of the game: To find the other half of your proverb.
Play action: Each index card has half of a proverb written on one half and the remaining portion written on the other. Players draw a half-card from the hat and try to find the other half with the completed proverb.
Hints and tips: Suggested list of proverbs:

1. Forewarned	is forearmed.
2. He who hesitates	is lost.
3. Beauty is	only skin deep.
4. All is not gold	that glitters.
5. A watched pot	never boils.
6. You can't make a silk purse	out of a sow's ear.
7. The last straw	break's the camel's back.
8. Set a thief	to catch a thief.
9. In for a penny	in for a pound.
10. One good turn	deserves another.
11. Every cloud has	a silver lining.
12. Absence makes the heart	grow fonder.
13. Necessity is the	mother of invention.
14. A bird in the hand	is worth two in the bush.
15. Jack of all trades	master of none.
16. Make hay while	the sun shines.
17. Familiarity	breeds contempt.
18. Time and tide	wait for no man.
19. A rolling stone	gathers no moss.
20. You can't eat your cake	and have it too.
21. Brevity is the	soul of wit.
22. A stitch in time	saves nine.
23. The pen is mightier	than the sword.
24. Spare the rod	and spoil the child.
25. Too many cooks	spoil the broth.
26. It takes two	to tango.
27. A friend in need	is a friend indeed.
28. Two wrongs do not	make a right.
29. There's no fool	like an old fool.
30. Look before	you leap.
31. The child is	father to the man.

32. A miss is as good	as a mile.
33. You can't burn the candle	at both ends.
34. Actions speak	louder than words.
35. Handsome is	as handsome does.
36. Children should be seen	and not heard.
37. Many hands make	light work.
38. Don't count your chickens	before they're hatched.
39. Out of sight	out of mind.
40. Half a loaf	is better than none.
41. When the cat's away	the mice will play.
42. Penny wise	and pound foolish.
43. Where there's a will	there's a way.
44. Still waters	run deep.
45. Nothing succeeds	like success.
46. A chain is as strong	as its weakest link.
47. One man's meat	is another man's poison.
48. All's fair	in love and war.
49. When in Rome	do as the Romans do.
50. Variety	is the spice of life.

Name of the game: Forming Partners.   **# of players:** Any.
Type: Forming couples.
Supplies: 3″x 5″ index cards, pencils. Hat or basket.
Formation: Mingling for pairing off.
Object of the game: To find a partner.
Play action: Each woman writes a description of herself and her clothes. The cards are mixed into a hat. Each man draws one card and looks for the woman described.
Adaptation: Vice versa.

Name of the game: Chinese Opera.   **# of players:** Any.
Type: Grouping.
Supplies: Prepare slips of paper with one or two lines written on separate slips. Have one for each guest.
Formation: Players mingle.
Object of the game: To find the people with the other lyrics belonging to your song.
Play action: Scatter the pieces of paper with the song lyrics on them in the middle of the floor. Each person takes a slip and then, having read his or her lyrics, tries to find the other lyrics belonging to that song.

FURTHER TIPS

Players draw cards and then try to find their partner or team members.

Twos:

- Famous couples, like Abbott and Costello,   Prince Charles and Lady Di,   Anthony and Cleopatra,   Beauty and Beast,   Duchess and Duke.
- Capitals and their corresponding states, such as Columbus and Ohio,   Little Rock and Arkansas,   Albany and New York.
- Foods, like bread and butter,   salt and pepper,   meat and potatoes,   pork and beans,   ice cream and cake.
- More pairs: paper and pencil,   thunder and lightning, soap and water,   stocks and bonds,   bow and arrow, lock and key,   cap and gown.

Threes:

- Papa Bear, Mama Bear, Baby Bear;   lock, stock, and barrel;   faith, hope, and charity;   army, navy, and air force; pennies, nickels, and quarters;   stop, caution, and go; Wynken, Blynken, and Nod;   red, white, and blue.

Fours:

- Family Portrait: An amusing way to divide your guests into groups of fours is to invent sets of family names, write these names on cards, pass them out, and let your guests find each other. One example: Admiral I.M. Murgatroyde, Ms. R.U. Murgatroyde, Miss B.B. Murgatroyde, Izzy Murgatroyde.

9
PARTY SUPPLIES & SAMPLE PLAN

SUPPLIES

As you read through the games-instructions chapters, you probably noticed that many games use some of the same basic materials. So why not buy a patterned-cloth or paper storage box with a lid, and as you collect supplies, save them in one place—your games box. This way, you will not have to scrounge up materials each time you have a party. Over time you can add to your box of supplies.

This is what a look into my games box reveals:

- alphabet "flash" cards (children's)
- dice
- pencils
- scissors
- string
- tennis balls
- a white bed sheet
- tape (transparent and masking)
- newspaper
- tacks
- decks of playing cards
- feathers
- beanbags
- index cards (3″ x 5″ and 4″ x 6″)

- soft-tipped pens
- patterns for making copies
- ribbon
- Ping-Pong balls
- straight and safety pins
- lunch bags
- navy beans
- poster board or cardboard
- good-quality balloons
- golf tees
- buttons
- pennies
- song titles
- peanuts

Since there are so many details to consider when entertaining, by having your supplies for games all together in one box, organization becomes much easier. When you are well into giving directions for a game, that is not the time to be hunting up tape, safety pins, or pencils.

Being able to distribute supplies quickly, either *before* or *after* giving instructions, is important, because people listen better when they can give their full attention. For example, if you are giving directions for a pencil-and-paper game and you want to show an example, pass out the prepared papers first and then proceed with the directions. On the other hand, if your game involves props, you may want to explain the game before the supplies are passed out. Of course, this means that you will have to select your games and plan your dispersal of supplies ahead of of time.

SAMPLE PLAN

· ·

The sample plan that follows will give you some concrete examples of how I do my own party planning. The occasion was an orientation meeting that I give every year for a student-exchange program; but, with various modifications, the plan could be applied to almost any other type of function.

The first thing I did was to devise the invitation.

EF HOST FAMILY ORIENTATION
& ICE CREAM SOCIAL

When: Saturday evening

August 13—7 P.M. to 10 P.M.

Where: Coronado Center
Hot Springs Village
(Maps at gate entrance)
*Bring: "Family Rules & Responsibilities" HF Handbook
*Bring: A topping for ice cream—nuts, sprinkles, M & M's,
etc. Drinks
(Attendance is required.)

This invitation could have been written on paper cut out in the shape of an ice-cream sundae.

Then I made out my plan.

Plan for Host Family Orientation

August 13, Sat. evening, 7:00 P.M.–10:00 P.M.
Ice-Cream Social
Members bring toppings and drinks.
Provide:

- Ice cream, bowls, spoons, coffee, Coca-Cola [√]
- Name-tag games [√]
- Balderdash-or-Not game (*see Chapter 6*) [√]
- Butcher paper and crayons (*A table will be covered in paper for the small children to draw a mural. Someone will sit with them during the lecture, and also provide quiet toys and games.*) [√]
- Quiet toys and games [√]
- Room rental [√]
- Coffeepot (*included in room rental*) [√]

- VCR and TV *(for tape presentation—also included in room rental, but you must ask for these services ahead of time)* [✓]
- Folders *(with materials and name tags)* [✓]
- Maps *(for the gate and/or future events)* [✓]
- Beforehand I will need to type:
  1. A Calendar of Events *(future planning for the year)* [✓]
  2. A Roster *(with all the families' names, addresses, and school affiliations)* [✓]
- Bring coffee [✓]
  - sugar [✓]
  - creamer [✓]
  - plastic spoons [✓]
  - liters of Coca-Cola [✓]
  - cups [✓]
  - tablecloth *(optional)* [✓]
- Reminder: Ask some of the members what toppings they will be bringing for the ice cream, so that we will not have too much of one thing. Suggested toppings:

  - fruit topping
  - broken Oreos
  - sprinkles
  - chocolate chips
  - nuts
  - whipped cream
  - candy
  - peanut butter chips

This may look like a lot of planning, but this affair was actually relatively simple for a few different reasons. First, the attendance was mandatory, so I knew my head count. The facilities were superior and I had used them before, so I knew what would be provided, like the blackboard and the television and VCR for my tape. It was also convenient having the coffeepot provided. The refreshments were the least of my problems, because the guests brought the toppings and I knew that if I bought the ice cream in large hard-packed-gallon sizes, it would be soft and just right for serving within the 3-hour time span. I bought one flavor: vanilla.

Providing the younger children with quiet games, drawing materials, and an attendant helped keep the noise down and freed up the parents to listen to the lecture.

The name tags were used as part of the entertainment, and you

saw that we used a Balderdash type of game. With this game, players select the correct definition of unusual words from five choices. I used this game to make a point: that although all the host families were well-versed in English, we too can misunderstand or misinterpret words, just as our foreign students might.

The orientation meeting went off without a hitch!

10
PARTY THEMES

The party themes that follow can be used as a springboard to get you to think up themes of your own. Remember, as Vladimir Nabokov says in *The Gift*: "Genius is an African who dreams up snow."

Party theme: Indoor Beach Party (for the winter blahs).
Invitations: Life preserver, bikini, fish, or beach-ball shapes. (On the invitation, you can suggest that guests wear shorts, T-shirts, and sneakers.)
Name tags: In the shape of palm trees or beach cabanas.
Decor: Lay around bottles of suntan lotion; have a well-lit fake sun. It's best if the party is confined to a recreation room, basement area, or indoor patio. Make a palm tree by wrapping brown crepe paper around a pole or pipe, and tie on large green paper "fronds" and real coconuts or pineapples to eat later. Hang fishnets and decorate them with fish scales and seashells. Lean a surfboard up against a wall. Lay plastic trash bags on the floor and top them with clean sand. Have a kiddie pool on the floor filled with water for your "ocean." Use lawn chairs and patio furniture for seating, and put up a cabana, real or otherwise. Leave sand pails and shovels out for playing.
Games: Limbo. A go-fishing setup in which players drop their line behind a screen and prizes or messages are "catch." If you have a lot of space, indoor volleyball with a soft spongelike ball. Any combination of other games and contests.
Gifts or prizes: Hawaiian shirts or T-shirts. Beach towels or lotion. Funny sunglasses.
Food: Grill hand-holder foods on the hibachi. Tropical fruits and drinks.
Music: Beach Boys, Frankie Avalon, Jan and Dean.

Party theme: Italian Dinner.

Invitations: Outline of Italy or a postcard of Italy. (Invitations can suggest that guests wear peasant dresses, aprons, kerchiefs, handlebar mustaches.)

Name tags: Mustache shapes or recipe cards.

Decor: Use red-checked tablecloths and napkins. Have candles burned over bottles. Hang the Italian flag and Italian travel posters. Leave out straw-covered Chianti bottles.

Games: Any drinking game (To Your Health, in Chapter 7, for example). Any combination of other games or hunts.

Gifts or prizes: The bottles of Chianti. Tins filled with spaghetti.

Food: Antipasto, pizza, garlic bread, spaghetti, bread sticks, cheese and fruit. Espresso coffee and chocolates.

Music: Opera, accordion, or other Italian music. You might even want to have a live accordion player or violinist to serenade tables.

Party theme: Mad Hatter's Tea.

Invitations: Shaped like Rabbit's top hat or Alice's potion bottle.

Name tags: To resemble Queen's cards, or other story details. You can play matching games with cards or with Tweedledum and Tweedledee characters.

Decor: Large posters or murals of the playing cards, Wonderland trees, the croquet setup, Rabbit's house. Large paper roses. (You can dress as Alice, with long blonde hair, white stockings, black patent-leather shoes, and a pinafore dress, or as Rabbit or the Cheshire Cat.)

Games: Pencil-and-paper games (hard ones), matching games, team contests, musical games.

Gifts or prizes: Teapots, decks of cards, tea in tins.

Food: Tea-party foods: crumpets, scones, muffins, fruit, and a selection of herbal and fruit teas. "Cheshire Mousse," "Queen of Hearts Tarts."

Music: Soundtrack from Disney's *Alice in Wonderland*, symphony music. Musical chairs music.

Party theme: 4th of July Barbecue.
Invitations: Red, white, and blue, or a military look.
Name tags: In the shape of firecrackers or the same as invitations above.
Decor: Flags, copies of the Bill of Rights, military or Uncle Sam posters. String lights in red, white, and blue for the evening.
Games: Relays and musical games.
Gifts or prizes: Miniature flags, camouflage hats, barbecue ware.
Food: Anything that is traditionally grilled. (Don't forget charcoal, kindling, matches, eating utensils, long forks, tongs, paper plates, and other paper products.)
Music: Military or patriotic music. Marches. Portable radio.

Party theme: April Fools.
Invitations: A social committee or a couple of friends make up the invitations, and a different invitation is sent to each couple or small group. For example, one group is told to dress in Western style, one to dress Hawaiian style, one in formal wear, one in togas, and so on.
Name tags: With cartoon characters from comic strips, or jesters.
Decor: Magic-trick items, mirrors. Harlequin designs.
Games: Lapse of Memory game (Chapter 5) and other icebreakers. Gags, stunts, and tricks.
Gifts or prizes: Comic or joke books; gag gifts like weighted dice, stacked decks of cards, and candles that don't blow out; novelty-shop items; fortune-telling eight balls.
Food: Decorate a stack of bricks to look like a beautiful cake. Real desserts, drinks, and coffee.
Music: Comedy routines, old radio shows, sound effects, potpourri of sound.

Party theme: Asian (perhaps Chinese New Year or "The Year of the Horse").
Invitations: Can be made to resemble a screen. Use rice paper or parchment. Write your message in free-flowing India-ink brush strokes. Make a small frame from popsicle sticks.
Name tags: Made to resemble kimonos.
Decor: Use predominantly black and white with a touch of red. Hang paper cutouts of dragons, temples, and broad swords. Decorate with Oriental fans and umbrellas too. For the table: Use a low table with pillow seating. Keep furniture groupings

sparse. Have flowers floating in bowls. Invite guests to remove their shoes at the door. Burn incense. Costumes: Possibly provide guests with Mandarin hats, thong sandals, and Chinese jackets with frogs, and wear them yourself.

Games: Table and pencil-and-paper games.

Gifts or prizes: Bonsai trees, chopsticks, fans.

Food: Rice, shrimp, sauces in small decorative bowls, wonton soup. Saki. Fortune cookies.

Music: Music from "Madam Butterfly" or traditional Asian music.

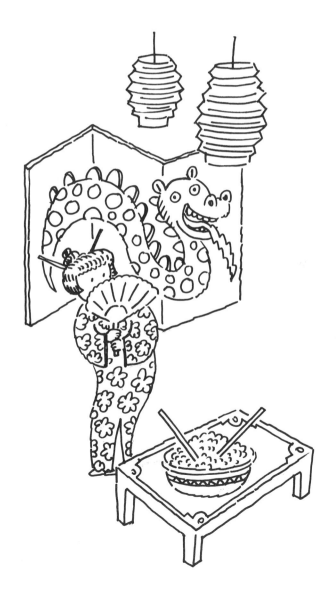

Party theme: Saloon Night.
Invitations: Shaped like cowboy boots and hats, or king and queen face cards. (Specify best Western dress, or flannel shirts, jeans, and boots.)
Name tags: A matching game for name tags using suits of cards.
Decor: Old lanterns, red-checked tablecloths, "Wanted" posters with drawings of guests. Water trough filled with water, gold glitter, and sand. Or a child's wading pool filled with water, BB pellets, and real gold beads. Pie pans for sifting. Sawdust, old bottles. Pewter and copper pots and vessels.
Game: Any card and card-related games. Contests and "panning for gold."
Gifts or prizes: Bubble-gum tobacco chew, gold chocolate coins. Cowboy hats and kerchiefs, fake turquoise jewelry. Beef jerky.
Food: Steak, salad, drinks. Popcorn, peanuts.
Music: Cowboy campfire songs or country-western music.

Party theme: Irish Gig.
Invitations: In the shape of a three- or four-leaf clover.
Name tags: Shaped like a leprechaun or any other good-luck symbol. Use phrases like "Top o' the Mornin' " and "Pot O' Gold."
Decor: Green everything. Blarney stone (stone washed and painted). Green hats and cutouts of clay pipes. Pot o' gold on buffet table, actually filled with gold chocolate coins.
Games: Contests and anything competitive. Weaving yarns and storytelling.
Gifts or prizes: Green jelly beans; live shamrock plants.
Food: Corned beef and cabbage, potatoes. Green jello salad. Whiskey and Irish coffee.
Music: Irish ballads.

Party theme: Valentine Romance.

Invitations: Red hearts with lace paper doilies.

Name tags: Heart shapes that are divided in half differently from all the rest, for a couples' matching game.

Decor: Valentines and ribbon. Red and pink tablecloth and candles. Heart-shaped boxes.

Games: Any couples games, bridging over to team games.

Gifts or prizes: Sachets, heart photo frames, Valentine candy. Take Polaroids of couples and place them in acrylic frames for mementos.

Foods: Valentine cake and punch. One cake baked square; another baked round. Cut the round one in half, piece it to the square cake, and you have a heart (see opposite page).

Music: Johnny Mathis, Nat King Cole.

To make a heart cake:

Bake one cake in a round pan, the other in a square pan.

Let cool on rack.

Cut round cake in half.

Piece together and frost.

Party theme: Mother's Day.

Invitations: Copy a line from a beautiful poem and attach real pressed flowers.

Decor: Breakfast in bed on a tray, with a flower and the newspaper. (Absolutely no dishes to be washed by Mother today.)

Games: Photo-album-page creation, done by the family. Shower games. Fashion a corsage.

Gift: Bathrobe or bed jacket; sachets.

Food: Waffles and champagne with fruit; coffee.

Music: Play music from your mother's young-adult years: Sinatra?

Alternative: Several women can arrange a Fashion Show Luncheon at a local hotel, or perhaps a poetry reading with dessert and coffee.

Party theme: Father's Day.
Invitations: Phone some family members or a few of Dad's friends.
Decor: Manly, sports stuff. Hang hubcaps or set up auto license plates. Set out model cars and planes.
Games: Tough Guy (in Chapter 7) and a combination of contests and stunts. You could give a speech—"Why Fathers Are More Valuable Today" or "Why Dad Is Still Cool."
Gifts or prizes: Crossword-puzzle magazines, beer mugs, football-team-logo goods.
Food: Stick-to-the-rib food, like chili or stew. Serve with crackers or crusty bread. Beer.
Music: College fight songs.

Party theme: Housewarming.
Invitations: On paper that looks like a blueprint or shaped like a tool.
Name tags: Shaped like an apron.
Decor: Friend's house—either under construction or just finished.
Games: Any suited for large, empty rooms. Musical.
Gifts or prizes: Gifts for the house: broom, mop, tools, cleaning supplies, gags.
Food: Box lunches or sandwiches. Pizza or fried chicken. Chips and hard-boiled eggs, apples. Soft drinks.
Music: Anything with a driving beat.

Party theme: Fiesta (Spanish Saint's Day).
Invitations: In the shape of a sombrero or a Spanish guitar, with wording like "Mucho gusto fun and laughs, Amigo."
Name tags: In the shape of red chili peppers.
Decor: Spanish travel posters and sombreros on the walls. Bright striped shawls draped over chairs. Piñatas. Guitars and castanets.
Games: Travel and music games, as well as any others.
Gifts or prizes: Fiesta-ware bowls; gaily painted ornaments with a Spanish flavor.
Food: Nachos. Mexican food and Spanish rice. Coronado beer with lime, or tequila with salt and lemons. Margaritas.
Music: Rumbas, cha-cha, lambadas, merengue. Or, for a change of pace, music from the opera *Carmen*.

When devising your own theme,

- keep it simple
- start the theme with the invitations
- rely on music
- invite input from everyone
- have fun!

In the winter, parties can center around activities like skiing, sleigh rides, ice skating, ice fishing, outdoor hot tubs, or hiking. Play active games and serve hot food such as baked casseroles, beef broth, and roast steaks. Make hot chocolate or rum toddies.

Other times of the year, parties can revolve around the beach, barges and boating, swimming, hiking, volleyball, biking, and cookouts of all kinds (doesn't food taste better in the open?).

More Ideas for a Variety of Parties and Events:

- Progressive dinners
- Cooking class
- Strawberry or watermelon festival
- Making ice cream
- Making ornaments, gifts, or bazaar items
- Teaching folk, square, or round dances
- Poetry reading
- Board-game rounds or championships
- Pinochle or bridge
- Quilting group (play word and thinking games)
- Seminar or workshop
- Viewing films
- Making a video
- Bon Voyage party
- Travel club get-togethers
- Literary or book-review club
- Bazaar or fundraiser
- Bake sale or car wash
- Wine and cheese party
- Anniversaries
- Housewarming or new-business ribbon cutting
- Crafts show or arts festival
- Medley events: contests, juggling, music, instructions, samples, clowns, mime
- Cocktail mixer
- Sleigh or hay ride
- Decorating a Christmas tree
- Christmas caroling
- Christmas baking
- Auction
- Staged productions: kidnapping or magic
- Charity, for flood victims, etc.
- Carnivals

- Audubon or hiking event
- Scrapbook party
- Showers
- Water events: beach, pool, or lake
- Party cruise
- Buggy ride in city

- Community cleanup
- "Olympics"
- Bingo
- Special suppers: chili, spaghetti, pancake, etc.
- Hawaiian luau

11
PRIZES & GIFTS

In her book, *Living a Beautiful Life,* Alexandra Stoddard says, "Think of your gift-giving as bringing an unexpected pleasure to someone you care about. An element of surprise intensifies satisfaction." Prizes and gifts for parties don't have to be expensive and they are not meant to be the "end all"—the latest or the greatest. If you give a secret family recipe tucked inside a recipe card file, you're enhancing someone's life. If the prize is a surprise and reflects the theme, then so much the better. Have fun with giving and learn to receive graciously as well.

What follows is a list of items that would be fun to give and receive.

SUGGESTIONS FOR GIFTS AND PRIZES

- specialty tea bags and teacup
- teapot
- coffee beans and coffee mug
- baskets
- fabric-covered boxes
- potpourri or sachets
- decorative soaps
- notepaper
- picture frames
- cookie cutters
- recipes and recipe cards
- lazy Susan
- sewing-repair kit
- lipstick and mirror
- bottle of wine or sangria

- book (blank or other)
- small flowering plant
- chocolates
- pepper mill
- seashells
- storage boxes
- American flag
- nail-polish kit
- museum postcards
- horoscope paperback
- decorative pencils
- sample cosmetics/perfumes
- votive candle and holder
- magnets
- fans
- Christmas ornaments

- perfume/cologne
- tins (decorative)
- sugar-and-creamer set
- playing cards
- hand-held games
- elegant room spray
- address book
- stationery
- old movie video
- collectible spoons
- watering can
- straw hat
- vase
- water pitcher

FOR SPECIAL CLUBS OR GROUPS

Garden club:
- garden gloves
- seed packets and tools
- planting apron
- plant pots and containers
- garden sculpture
- plant stakes
- vine cuttings

Sewing or craft group:
- scissors
- thread and card of buttons
- lace
- grosgrain ribbon
- trims
- pincushions and pins
- notions
- embroidery hoop
- tape measure
- paint brushes

- palette
- tubes of oils/watercolors

Camera club:
- film
- camera case
- photo album
- storage cases

Literary group:
- magnifying glass
- cloth book cover
- book plates
- vinyl cover for paperbacks
- bookmarks
- eyeglass case
- book light
- book of poems

Investment club:
- ledger
- change purse
- business-card holder
- calendar
- money clip
- calculator
- photo wallet

Audubon club:
- birdhouse
- seed
- outdoor thermometer
- small binoculars

Decorating group:
- magazine subscription
- tassels
- hand towels
- duster

- candlesticks
- chintz pillows

Sports clubs:
- tote bags
- umbrella
- golf balls and tees
- can of tennis balls
- baseball
- Frisbee
- sweat bands
- weights
- athletic shirts

- special socks
- lawn darts
- visor
- cleaning equipment

Picnic and barbecue friends:
- tongs
- aprons, mitts, and hats
- drink holders and straws
- plastic picnic ware
- homemade bread
- basket with condiments

DOOR PRIZES

Door prizes are fun for everyone and a great incentive for increasing club membership. If your club or association is on a budget, some stores will donate gifts for their endorsement. Often, if you tell a store that you will announce that an item was donated by them, they will be more than willing to help, and many stores actually have a budget allotted for this type of thing. Remember to acknowledge their generosity with a thank-you note, written on club letterhead, shortly after the event.

GIFTS FOR NONTRADITIONAL SHOWERS

Although bridal and baby showers are the most common, showers can be thrown for just about anyone. For example, you can hold a shower for a student who is going off to college. The shower gifts can be school supplies and everyone can play thinking games. What about a party for a friend who has adopted a new baby or an older child? Or you could start a new tradition of holding showers for friends starting a new business. The gifts in this case could be office supplies and small furnishing details. For a couple's first cruise, have a "knotty" shower, where all the items given are tied into knots, like towels and linens. To celebrate someone's award for "volunteer of the year," the gifts can

be supplies like serving trays, napkins, coasters, bar equipment, and confetti.

Parties where the guests make up scrapbooks or put mementos together in a file are perfect for a family member or friend moving away, or for a professional moving up in his or her field. What a wonderful gesture of love and support this can be.

GIFT-GIVING GAMES

We often play a game called "Pick-a-Gift, Steal-a-Gift." Everyone buys or makes an item in which the cost comes to less than five dollars. The gifts are wrapped and placed in a pile at the party. They are then retrieved alphabetically. For instance, the person whose name begins with *A* gets to go to the pile of gifts and select any item. As it is opened, the other players comment on its contents: "Great gift," "Good color," and so on. The next player, the person whose name begins with the next letter, in this case *B*, must then decide whether to steal the gift that player *A* has opened or go to the pile and select a new present. There is one rule of thumb: An item cannot be stolen more than three times. If an item is stolen from you—well, it's not so bad, because you get to select and open another. However, some people try to time it so that they can be last to steal a much-desired gift.

The game that follows is good for mixing as well as giving gifts.

Name of the game: Unique Gift-Giving.   **# of players:** Any.
Type: Gift game.
Supplies: Good-weight string; prizes.
Formation: Players mixing in a fairly large room. At the end of long pieces of string a small prize is tied. The strings are loosely wound in and out and around objects, perhaps around the legs of chairs and behind other furniture, forming a jumble of crisscrossing string. The strings should begin at the same starting point.
Object of the game: To uncover a small prize.
Play action: Players unravel strings to find and reveal prizes.

GIFT WRAPPING

The wrapping is an important element in giving gifts and prizes. We've all heard of people wrapping a small gift in a box and then putting that box into a larger box, wrapping that, and then putting it into a still larger box, and so on. This idea is probably just as entertaining for the onlookers as it is for the participant. It takes time, but it can be great fun.

Here are some other gift-wrapping ideas:

- Wrap a package in a page from a glossy magazine. For example, use a photo of a beautiful model for a cosmetics gift, or how about an automotive advertisement for car-care items?
- Use a map to wrap a "Bon Voyage" or "Welcome to the Neighborhood" gift.
- Wrap the package to resemble an animal or a face or another object like a house.

- Use a blowup of the company's name from the Yellow Pages for a company party gift.
- Use the comics section of the Sunday paper for the kid in all of us.
- Wrap the gift to play off on the recipient's name. For example, a package for Penny could have pennies taped all over it, and Wendy's gift could have the logo, cut out of the take-out bag from your local Wendy's restaurant, glued onto it.

GAMES BY CATEGORY

Artistic or Creative:
Cartoonists, 112–113
Dear Santa Claus, 81
Decorate a Banana, Potato, 113
Nursery Room Drawings, 109
Tell a Truth, 91
Van Gogh, 107

Contest:
Alliteration, 68
In the Bag, 56
False Observation, 82–83
Football Daffynitions, 86–87
Guess How Many, 61
Guess the Weight, 61
How Many, How Much?, 62–63
How Old?, 66
Item-by-Item Hunt, 114–115
Men vs. Women, 68
Signs and Signals, 64
Storyteller, 111
Tip the Orange, 65
True or False, 67
Where in the World?, 66
Wool Ravel, 64–65
Word Builders, 75
Words—More!, 106–107

Event:
Bunko, 115–117
Shogum, 118

Get-Acquainted:
Bean Dealer, 59–60
Beautiful Baby, 69
Couples' Quiz, 71
Finders Meeters, 56–57
First Impression, 56
Just Your Name, 71
Lapse of Memory, 77
Mix It Up, 72
Mystery Guest, 57
Name Bingo, 77–78
Sack Shake, 71
Tell a Truth, 91
What's New?, 58

Gift Exchange:
Steal-a-Gift, 93
Unique Gift Giving, 148

Grouping:
Chinese Opera, 121
Forming Partners, 121
Proverb Mate, 120–121
Three of a Kind, 119

Guessing:
In the Bag, 56
Bean Dealer, 59–60
Beautiful Baby, 69
False Observation, 82–83
Feelings, 76–77

153

Football Daffynitions, 86–87
Guess How Many, 61
Guess the Weight, 61
How Many, How Much?, 62–63
How Old?, 66
Mixed-Up Mottos, 89
Signs and Signals, 64
What's in a Name?, 70
Wink (or Murder), 88

Hunt:
Item-by-Item Hunt, 114–115
Sentence-Clue Hunt, 114
Shogum, 118
String Along, 58–59

Icebreakers:
Bean Dealer, 59–60
Beautiful Baby, 69
Couples' Quiz, 71
Feelings, 76–77
Finders Meeters, 56–57
First Impression, 56
Guess How Many, 61
Guess the Weight, 61
How Many, How Much?, 62–63
Just Your Name, 71
Lapse of Memory, 77
Men vs. Women, 68
Mix It Up, 72
Mystery Guest, 57
Name Bingo, 77–78
Personal Bingo, 72
Pocket Hunt, 72–73
Proverb Mate, 120–121
Sack Shake, 71
Sentence Mix-Ups, 74–75
Signs and Signals, 64
Three of a Kind, 119
What's in a Name?, 70
What's New?, 58
Word Builders, 75

Music:
Music Me a Balloon, 101
Penny Ante, 94
Singing Charades, 82
To Your Health, 104

Pencil-and-Paper:
Balderdash or Not, 84–85
Cartoonists, 112–113
Connected-Word Thinking, 88
Dear Advice Columnist, 112
Dear Santa Claus, 81
Desert Island Among Friends, 80
False Observation, 82–83
Football Daffynitions, 86–87
Hidden Cities, 83
How Old?, 66
Mixed-Up Mottos, 89
Newspaper Reporter, 89
Numbers Are, 90
Nursery Room Drawings, 109
One-Minute Words, 112
Personal Favorites, 80
Resolutions (New Year's), 91
Ridiculous, 85
The Robust Letter, 87
Singing Charades, 82
Slogans for the Famous, 111
Telegram, 87
Van Gogh, 107
Where in the World?, 66
Words—More!, 106–107

Physical or Active:
Bunko, 115–117
Chinese Opera, 121
Chin-to-Chin, 96
Crazy Bowling, 99
Feathers, 107
Fish-Pool Relay, 100
Forming Partners, 121

Item-by-Item Hunt, 114–115
Music Me a Balloon, 101
Pass the Orange, 95
Ping-Pong Blow, 92
Playing-Card Race, 100
Proverb Mate, 120–121
Roll Along, 98
Sentence-Clue Hunt, 114
Sentence Mix-Ups, 74–75
Shogum, 118
Socks and Gloves, 103
Spoons, 97
Steal-a-Gift, 93
String Along, 58–59
Three of a Kind, 119
Tip the Orange, 65
Tough Guy, 103
True or False, 67
Variety Relay, 98
Waiter Please, 98–99
Winner, 100–101
Word Builders, 75

Pre-party:
In the Bag, 56
Bean Dealer, 59–60
Feelings, 76–77
Finders Meeters, 56–57
First Impression, 56
Guess How Many, 61
Guess the Weight, 61
How Many, How Much?, 62–63
Mystery Guest, 57
Signs and Signals, 64
String Along, 58–59
Tip the Orange, 65
What's New?, 58
Wool Ravel, 64–65

Quick Thinking:
Alliteration, 68
Chinese Opera, 121

Dear Advice Columnist, 112
Men vs. Women, 68
Proverb Mate, 120–121
Sentence Mix-Ups, 74–75
Slogans for the Famous, 111
Sneaky Sentences, 110–111
Three of a Kind, 119
True or False, 67

Showers:
Cartoonists, 112–113
Dear Advice Columnist, 112
Decorate a Banana, Potato, 113
Diaper Cross, 110
Nursery Room Drawings, 109
One-Minute Words, 112
Slogans for the Famous, 111
Sneaky Sentences, 110–111
Storyteller, 111

Skill or Task:
Crazy Bowling, 99
Decorate a Banana, Potato, 113
Diaper Cross, 110
Driver's Test, 104–105
Fish-Pool Relay, 100
Men vs. Women, 68
Pass the Orange, 95
Roll Along, 98
Sentence-Clue Hunt, 114
Singing Charades, 82
Sneaky Sentences, 110–111
Socks and Gloves, 103
Storyteller, 111
Tip the Orange, 65
Tough Guy, 103
Van Gogh, 107
Variety Relay, 98
Waiter Please, 98–99
Walk the Line, 104
Wink (or Murder), 88

Winner, 100–101
To Your Health, 104

Table:
Map It Out, 93
Penny Ante, 94
Ping-Pong Blow, 92
Resolutions (New Year's), 91
Steal-a-Gift, 93

Teams:
Alliteration, 68
Chin-to-Chin, 96
Connected-Word Thinking, 88
Crazy Bowling, 99
Desert Island Among Friends,
  80
Feathers, 107
Fish-Pool Relay, 100
Hidden Cities, 83
How Old?, 66
Map It Out, 93
Men vs. Women, 68
Pass the Orange, 95
Ping-Pong Blow, 92
Playing-Card Race, 100

Roll Along, 98
Shogum, 118
Signs and Signals, 64
Singing Charades, 82
String Along, 58–59
Tip the Orange, 65
Tough Guy, 103
True or False, 67
Variety Relay, 98
Waiter Please, 98–99
Where in the World?, 66
Winner, 100–101
Wool Ravel, 64–65
Word Builders, 75
Words—More!, 106–107

Word:
Balderdash or Not, 84–85
Connected-Word Thinking, 88
"Dis" and "De," 79
Hidden Cities, 83
Newspaper Reporter, 89
One-Minute Words, 112
The Robust Letter, 87
Telegram, 87
Word Builders, 75
Words—More!, 106–107

INDEX

A

active games, 95–101
Alliteration, 68
April Fools party, 132
Asian party, 132–133
assistants, use of, 40–42
atmosphere for party, 13–14, 25–33
attention, signal for, 36
Audubon club, gifts and prizes
  for, 145

B

baby shower games, 109–110
Balderdash or Not, 84–85
barbecue, gifts and prizes for, 146
Bean Dealer, 59–60
Beautiful Baby, 69
bridal shower games, 110–113
Bunko, 115–117

C

camera club, gifts and prizes for, 145
candles, 29–30
Cartoonists, 112–113
Chinese New Year party, 132–133
Chinese Opera, 121
Chin-to-Chin, 96
clubs or groups, gifts and prizes for,
  145–146
Connected-Word Thinking, 88
contests, 61–68. *See also specific
  contests*
Couples' Quiz, 71
craft club, gifts and prizes for, 145
Crazy Bowling, 99

D

Dear Advice Columnist, 112
Dear Santa Claus, 81
Decorate a Banana, Potato, 113
decorating group, gifts and prizes
  for, 145–146

D (cont.)

decorations, 29–31
Desert Island Among Friends, 80
Diaper Cross, 110
door prizes, 146
drinking game, 104
Driver's Test, 104–105

E

events, 115–118

F

False Observation, 82–83
Father's Day, 139
Feathers, 107
Feelings, 76–77
Fiesta party, 139
Finders Meeters, 56–57
First Impression, 56
Fish-Pool Relay, 100
flowers, 29
Football Daffynitions, 86–87
forfeit games, 103–107, 111
formations for games, 40
Forming Partners, 121
4th of July Barbecue, 132
furniture arrangement, 29

G

games box, 123
garden club, gifts and prizes for, 145
get-acquainted games, 59–60. *See
  also specific games*
gift-giving games, 93, 148
gifts, 143–146, 148
gift wrapping, 150–151
grouping or pairing, 119–122
Guess How Many, 61
guessing games, 56, 59–64. *See also
  specific guessing games*
Guess the Weight, 61

H

Hidden Cities, 83
Housewarming, 139
How Many, How Much?, 62–63
How Old?, 66
hunts, 114–115. *See also specific hunts*

I

icebreakers, 69–77. *See also specific icebreakers*
Indoor Beach Party, 129
instructions for games, giving, 37
In the Bag, 56
investment club, gifts and prizes for, 145
invitations, 16–23
Irish Gig, 135
Italian Dinner, 131
Item-by-Item Hunt, 114–115

J

Just Your Name, 71

L

Lapse of Memory, 77
leadership techniques, 35–37
lighting, 29
literary group, gifts and prizes for, 145
locations for parties, 26–28

M

Mad Hatter's Tea, 131
Map It Out, 93
material for games, knowledge of, 37
Men vs. Women, 68
Mixed-Up Mottos, 89
Mix It Up, 72
Mother's Day, 138
motivating your guests, 45–54
musical activities, 82, 94, 101, 104
Music Me a Balloon, 101
Mystery Guest, 57

N

Name Bingo, 77–78
Newspaper Reporter, 89
Numbers Are, 90
Nursery Room Drawings, 109

O

One-Minute Words, 112

P

pairing or grouping, 119–122
party planning
  invitations, 16–23
  questions to ask yourself, 14–16
  setting and mood, 13–14
party themes, 129–141
  April Fools, 132
  Asian, 132–133
  Father's Day, 139
  Fiesta (Spanish Saint's Day), 139
  4th of July Barbecue, 132
  Housewarming, 139
  Indoor Beach Party, 129
  Irish Gig, 135
  Italian Dinner, 131
  Mad Hatter's Tea, 131
  Mother's Day, 138
  Saloon Night, 134
  Valentine Romance, 136
Pass the Orange, 95
Pencil-and-paper games, 81–89. *See also specific pencil-and-paper games*
Penny Ante, 94
Personal Bingo, 72
Personal Favorites, 80
picnic, gifts and prizes for, 146
Ping-Pong Blow, 92
plan, sample, 125–127
Playing-Card Race, 100
Pocket Hunt, 72–73
potluck, 32–33
pre-party games, 55–78. *See also specific pre-party games*
prizes, 143–146
progress of game, assessment of, 37
Proverb Mate, 120–121

Q

questions, 37
quiet, waiting for, 36
quiet games, 81–91. *See also specific quiet games*

R

relays, 95–101. *See also specific relays*
Resolutions (New Year's), 91
Ridiculous, 85
The Robust Letter, 87
Roll Along, 98

S

Sack Shake, 71
Saloon Night, 134
sample plan, 125–127
scents, 30
Sentence-Clue Hunt, 114
Sentence Mix-Ups, 74–75
sewing club, gifts and prizes for, 145
Shogum, 118
shower games, 109–113
signal for attention, 36
Signs and Signals, 64
Singing Charades, 82
Slogans for the Famous, 111
Sneaky Sentences, 110–111
Socks and Gloves, 103
Spanish Saint's Day, 139
Spoons, 97
sports club, gifts and prizes for, 146
Steal-a-Gift, 93
Storyteller, 111
String along, 58–59
stunts, 103–105, 107
supplies, 123–124

T

table games, 91–94
tableware, 31
team games, 95–96, 100–101. *See
also specific team games*

Telegram, 87
Tell a Truth, 91
themes, party, 129–141
timing for games, 38–40
Tip the Orange, 65
Tough Guy, 103
To Your Health, 104
traffic flow, 32
True or False, 67

U

Unique Gift Giving, 148

V

Valentine Romance party, 136–137
Van Gogh, 107
Variety Relay, 98
visibility of leader, 35

W

Waiter Please, 98–99
Walk the Line, 104
What's in a Name?, 70
What's New?, 58
Where in the World?, 66
Wink (or Murder), 88
Winner, 100–101
Wool Ravel, 64–65
Word Builders, 75
Words—More!, 106–107